D1799245

HOUSING POLICY

A CONSULTATIVE DOCUMENT

*Presented to Parliament by the
Secretary of State for the Environment
and the Secretary of State for Wales
by Command of Her Majesty
June 1977*

LONDON
HER MAJESTY'S STATIONERY OFFICE
£2.50 net

Cmnd. 6851

ISBN 0 10 168510 6

Contents

FOREWORD
by the Secretary of State for the Environment and the
Secretary of State for Wales

Since 1975, the Department of the Environment and the Welsh Office have been engaged upon a thoroughgoing review of housing policy in England and Wales.

Any review of housing must be governed by a proper sense of its importance to both the community and the individual. As a nation we have wisely recognised this over the years. Housing policy is not simply about finance and resources; it is about homes for people.

Housing provokes intense debate; and rightly so. It affects everyone. But it is a commentary on our times that housing is often discussed as though things were getting worse, when the facts do not support this view. We are better housed as a nation than ever before; and our standards of housing seem to compare well with those of similar and more prosperous countries. This should give pause to critics who start with an assumption that present arrangements have served and are serving us badly.

Nevertheless, the rising housing standards of the great majority contrast sharply and starkly with those of people still living in poor or unsuitable housing. There are the people who still live in slums, in houses lacking basic amenities, in overcrowded conditions, or who have to share against their will and in difficult circumstances. There are those of our fellow-citizens with special housing needs, such as the elderly, the disabled and the handicapped. And there are those who are homeless. In addition there is the problem of whole neighbourhoods in our inner cities which are weighed down with concentrations of bad housing. So where should we go from here?

We and our colleagues believe that we should adopt a more selective and discerning approach to housing policy—one which will ensure that the most pressing housing needs of individuals and areas are tackled effectively and urgently, whilst at the same time making it easier for more people, and their children as they grow up, to get the kind of home they want. But we certainly do not believe that the household budgets of millions of families—which have been planned in good faith in the reasonable expectation that present arrangements would broadly continue—should be overturned, in pursuit of some theoretical or academic dogma.

This is a consultative document. There is now the opportunity for everyone to advance and to argue their views on housing policy. We hope that the Green Paper and its supporting technical volume of descriptive and analytical material will provide the basis for a better informed debate on housing policy than ever before.

Introductory Note

1 This consultation document is the outcome of a comprehensive review of housing policy in England and Wales which began early in 1975.*

2 The Review was initially confined largely to financial issues†. But it became clear that to restrict the Review in this way would diminish its usefulness, and so it was decided to widen its scope to include social aspects of housing. It was also decided that certain issues affecting the private rented sector called for separate examination. A Review of the Rent Acts was therefore started and a consultation document was issued in January this year.

3 The work of the Housing Policy Review was supported by several committees of experts on housing matters drawn from outside Government—by an Advisory Group on general issues, and Advisory Groups on Housing Services and other specific subjects.† The views expressed in the Green Paper are those of the Government, and do not necessarily represent the views of individual members of the Advisory Group or the other specialist groups.

4 The Government received a great deal of helpful evidence from interested bodies and individuals.†

5 Several official studies of relevance to housing policy have been in progress over the last year or two:

—following the report of the Committee of Inquiry into Local Government Finance (the Layfield Report, Cmnd 6453) last year, a Green Paper on Local Government Finance was published in May 1977 (Cmnd 6813);

—the Government announced in autumn 1976 their intention to undertake a review of the problems of inner city areas, taking account of the inner area studies which have been in progress for the last four years, and a White Paper, 'Policy for the Inner Cities' (Cmnd 6845), was published in June;

—the Government announced in September 1976 their intention of undertaking a reappraisal of new town programmes as part of the review of decentralisation policy. A statement was made to the House of Commons on 5 April 1977;

—a consultation document on transport policy was published in April 1976, and following wide ranging consultations the Government published a White Paper in June this year (Cmnd 6836).

All these studies, as well as consultations on the Green Paper itself, will be taken into account in moving towards conclusions on future housing policy later in the year.

---

*A review of housing finance in Scotland has been carried out by the Scottish Office in parallel with the present Review. Its report is being published separately.

†The original terms of reference, memberships of advisory bodies, and a list of the main submissions received are given in Annex A.

6 The Green Paper is intended to be reasonably self-contained. But detailed descriptive and analytical material produced in the course of the Review will also be published in a separate volume, the contents of which are set out in Annex C.

7 The Government intend to hold consultations on the main proposals with all the major interested parties. Those who wish to comment on the proposals should write to the Department of the Environment, Room N11/07, 2 Marsham Street, London SW1P 3EB, by 1 November 1977. This will allow a period of about 4 months for consultation before the Government reach firm conclusions on future policy.

Part I: The Framework for a Housing Policy

CHAPTER 1

The Starting Point

1.1 The Government believe that all families should be able to obtain a decent home at a price within their means. This has been the dominant theme of post-war housing policy. Although the emphasis has changed from time to time, the objective has remained the same. We have gone a long way towards realising this traditional objective; housing conditions have been greatly improved in the last 25 years, and millions of families have benefited. But serious problems remain. The Government will therefore continue to give a high priority to housing.

1.2 Since the Government took office in March 1974, new directions in housing policy have been pursued:

—following the Housing Act 1974, there has been a shift away from large schemes of clearance and redevelopment and a new emphasis on area improvement and renewal;

—the Housing Act 1974 also gave new impetus to the growth of housing associations as an alternative source of housing;

—the Rent Act 1974 freed hundreds of thousands of tenants in furnished accommodation from the fear of arbitrary eviction by giving them full security of tenure;

—a start has been made on stabilising the flow of mortgages for home ownership by the £500m short term loans provided by Government to the building societies in 1974; by the development of voluntary stabilisation arrangements by the Government and the building societies; and by the negotiation by the Government of 'support' mortgage lending by the building societies to supplement direct lending by local authorities*;

—the Housing Rents and Subsidies Act 1975 gave back to local authorities the freedom to fix rents which was withdrawn by the Conservative Government's Housing Finance Act 1972, and included provisions to enable local authorities and housing associations to set up housing co-operatives;

—the Rent (Agriculture) Act 1976 ended the insecurity of the tied cottage system, from which farm workers have suffered for generations;

—the Government prepared legislation which places the primary responsibility for dealing with homelessness on local authorities, and are supporting a Private Member's Bill to give effect to this;

—local authorities have been given flexibility in the use of public sector resources in 1977/78 as the first step towards the introduction of Housing Investment Programmes in 1978/79.

---

*'Local authority' is the term normally used in the Green Paper to describe local *housing* authorities.

1

The Government now intend to develop a comprehensive policy for housing which they hope will be durable enough to last for many years to come.

1.3 Success in overcoming our present economic difficulties is fundamental in generating more resources for the future. But resources will always be limited. We shall never be able to move forward on all fronts as fast as we would wish. This means that—in housing as in other fields—it is important to make the most of available resources. Housing policy does not exist in a vacuum. We must all recognise that the degree of priority to be given to housing has to be weighed against other claims not only for socially desirable expenditure but also for strengthening our industrial base.

1.4 Furthermore, housing policy affects our lives at so many points that it must be related to a wide range of other policies and issues:

—TRANSPORT AND EMPLOYMENT Housing, employment and transport are closely interconnected. Decisions on the location of new housing can have important implications for employment, and *vice versa*. Decisions on changes in transport facilities can affect housing and jobs. And in a period of rapid industrial change, the ease with which a worker can move house will assume increasing importance.

—PLANNING AND THE ENVIRONMENT Housing is a crucial factor in the changing form of towns. The planning system—including the Community Land Act—is closely concerned with the provision and availability of land for housing development, and there is an interaction between the planning system and housing policy, which influences the amount of new land required.

—INNER URBAN AREAS Many strands of policy come together in the consideration of the future of inner urban areas. These areas are not alone in having bad housing conditions. But the concentrations of such conditions in the inner urban areas are often associated with other severe social problems, especially poverty and unemployment. There has been wholesale demolition of older housing, accompanied by the disruption of existing communities and loss of jobs. An effective housing policy can play a central part in regenerating these areas.

—THE CONSTRUCTION INDUSTRY Housebuilding provides about 40 per cent of the new building workload of the construction industry. Housing policies which too often change direction are harmful to the efficiency of the industry and its suppliers, and lead to higher costs for the whole community. It is important to secure a reasonably stable level of demand for new and improved housing so that the industry does not suffer from periodic, damaging under-utilisation of its resources.

—SOCIAL WELFARE Housing policy cannot on its own deal with the particular problems, such as low income and infirmity, which make it difficult for some people to fend for themselves. But housing policy

2

must take account of the special needs of frail elderly people, the disabled and other exposed groups. Poverty and other disadvantages should not be allowed to condemn people to bad housing.

1.5 We must do our best to ensure that any new policy for housing works with and not across the grain of the Government's industrial, economic and social policies; and that it is internally coherent. This is easier said than done. For this reason, housing policy needs to be flexible enough to accommodate new and unexpected circumstances.

CHAPTER 2

The Objectives of Housing Policy

2.01 Some people consider that the housing situation today is paradoxical. Housing in England and Wales appears to compare reasonably well in terms of basic amenities and space with countries in both Western Europe and North America. We have more and better houses* in relation to the number of households than ever before. Nevertheless, despite a sharp rise in total housing expenditure in recent years, problems persist. Housing is sometimes discussed as though little has been achieved and things are getting worse.

2.02 The explanation of the paradox may lie in the widening gap between the majority living in housing of good standard and the substantial but diminishing number living in poor conditions; and in the fact that the inflation of recent years resulted in increases in average payments by householders in line with or faster than prices—though not normally as much as earnings—*despite* big increases in general assistance.†

THE PRESENT SITUATION

2.03 The main conclusions reached in Part II of the Green Paper, which provide the essential background to the Government's housing objectives, are summarised below.

Housing Conditions

2.04 In 1951, there were nearly 10 million households in England and Wales—families with children, childless couples, and people on their own—living in physically unsatisfactory conditions or sharing accommodation. By 1976 the figure had probably fallen to about 2·7 million and there was no longer an absolute shortage of houses. These figures are a cause for both satisfaction and concern: satisfaction that so much has been done; concern that much remains to be done. The continuing improvement in national housing conditions is no consolation to people who remain in poor conditions. On the contrary, their problems are thrown into sharp relief.

2.05 The national total of 2·7 million conceals almost as much as it reveals. It undoubtedly includes substantial numbers of households living in circumstances which most people would not accept for their own families—this may apply to not less than one household in ten (about 1·8 million)—but it covers a wide spectrum, ranging from households living in houses which are seriously substandard or overcrowded to households who are willingly sharing accommodation of good standard.

---

*'House' is the term used throughout the Green Paper for all types of accommodation except where a distinction is explicitly made between houses, flats, etc.

†'General assistance' is the term used in the Green Paper to describe tax relief on mortgage interest or option mortgage subsidy for house purchasers; Exchequer housing subsidies to the public sector which are not directly related to tenants' incomes; and General Rate Fund contributions to local authorities' Housing Revenue Accounts. It is not used to cover rent rebates for public sector tenants, rent allowances for private tenants, rate rebates, or supplementary benefit.

2.06 But national figures do not show that some areas have been left behind by the general improvement in housing standards, especially in the inner cities, where there are concentrations of run down housing and the problems are compounded by other social and economic difficulties. Furthermore, conventional definitions of unsatisfactory housing conditions do not bring into the reckoning:

—households living in houses which are technically neither unfit nor substandard but which are in a serious state of disrepair—many of these households are elderly people living on their own;

—households living in housing which is physically sound but unsuited to their needs—for example, families with small children living in flats above ground level;

—the difficult problems that some people face in getting suitable housing.

2.07 If present trends continue there will be substantial further progress in dealing with the backlog of bad housing conditions as well as providing for new households. Projections* made for the Review show various ways in which this might come about. But these projections are not firm forecasts; and they cannot take account of important and unpredictable changes that might occur. Furthermore, national projections of current trends tell us little about the right balance to be struck between the provision of new housing and the improvement of existing housing, about how particular groups will fare, or what progress will be made in areas with the most difficult housing problems.

2.08 We can only establish precisely how much needs to be done, where, and when, by local assessment. But clearly rehabilitation and repair, and better management and use of the housing stock, will often be just as important as new housebuilding in dealing with bad housing conditions and providing for new households.

2.09 Special issues affecting the continuing contraction of the private rented sector will be further considered in the Review of the Rent Acts.

Housing Finance

2.10 In recent years, big and rapid increases in house and land prices, construction costs, and interest rates subjected the financing of housing to unprecedented strains. The house price explosion of 1971–73 pulled local authority tender prices up with it. An important contributory factor was the scale of lending by the building societies and other lending agencies. Price increases were followed by very large increases in interest rates needed to get domestic credit back under control. The supply of mortgage funds dropped sharply and the level of new investment in housebuilding for home-ownership was therefore disrupted. Nevertheless, investment in the construction and improvement of housing in the public sector rose.

---

*Technical Volume, Chapter 3.

2.11 The impact of rising costs on public sector tenants and mortgagors was moderated by substantial increases in general assistance, which grew much faster than investment. Consequently, over the period 1971/72 to 1975/76 unrebated rents of public sector tenants and housing payments of home owners rose on average at about the same rate as prices generally. But there were periods when in both main sectors average payments by householders increased more than prices, and even exceeded increases in earnings.

2.12 A large part of the increase in housing costs in recent years resulted from successive rises in interest rates. If interest rates were to stabilise or fall, less general assistance would be required. But the events of the first half of the nineteen seventies underline the need to develop arrangements which will minimise the disruptive effects on housing of short-term changes in economic and financial conditions.

Pricing and Assistance

2.13 The question of the price people should pay for housing cannot be settled by a simple formula. Many young families opt to become home owners although —even with the help of mortgage tax relief*—they may initially have to devote more than a fifth of their net income to mortgage payments. On the other hand the poorest families can afford little for their housing without going short of other necessities.

2.14 The Government have considered various alternatives to the present arrangements for the pricing of housing and general assistance, such as the introduction of pricing related to current values in the owner-occupied and public rented sectors, the elimination or substantial reduction of general assistance, and a 'universal housing allowance'. But the price and supply of housing are related. Any change which would substantially raise the cost of housing to the house-holder in relation to prices and incomes generally would probably lead to a large reduction in housing investment. And the decisions and family budgets of millions of households have been shaped by the expectation that existing arrangements will continue in broadly their present form.

2.15 The present basis of pricing and general assistance can be criticised as tending to encourage excessive consumption of housing. But the case for alter-native arrangements must be weighed against the diversion of some expenditure currently devoted to housing into other channels and the need for wider use of income-related assistance and very complex administrative machinery. Over the years the view has been held that the well-being of present and future generations is better safeguarded if housing is not left solely to market forces. The Govern-ment believe that this remains a wise judgment, and that it is right to maintain:

---

*'Mortgage tax relief' includes option mortgage subsidy unless otherwise stated.

—the present system of pricing in the owner-occupied and public rented sectors, based on costs actually incurred,* not hypothetical current values;

—income-related assistance for tenants with lower incomes;

—general assistance with housing costs in the owner-occupied and public rented sectors.

HOUSING OBJECTIVES

2.16   The Government believe that the objectives of housing policy must be rooted in the traditions and reasonable expectations of the nation, but must also reflect present realities. In the light of the conclusions on the present housing situation, the Government propose that policy for housing over the next decade should be directed towards the following objectives:—

(i) The traditional aim of a decent home for all families at a price within their means must remain our primary objective Many families are still living in unsatisfactory housing conditions. But we should no longer think about this only in terms of national totals. This may have made sense when there was an overwhelming absolute shortage of housing everywhere. It makes sense no longer. On the contrary, a national approach can draw attention and resources away from the areas with the most pressing needs.

(ii) We must try to secure a better balance between investment in new houses and the improvement and repair of older houses, with regard to the needs of the individual and the community, as well as to cost.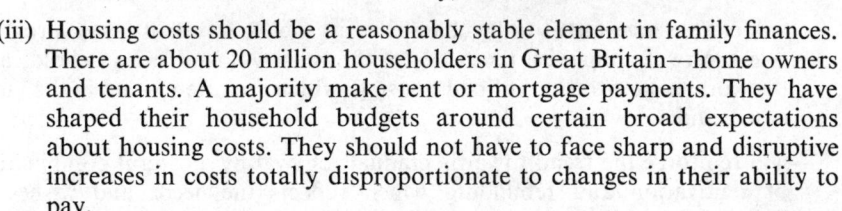

(iii) Housing costs should be a reasonably stable element in family finances. There are about 20 million householders in Great Britain—home owners and tenants. A majority make rent or mortgage payments. They have shaped their household budgets around certain broad expectations about housing costs. They should not have to face sharp and disruptive increases in costs totally disproportionate to changes in their ability to pay.

(iv) We must ensure that the housing needs of groups such as frail elderly people, the disabled and the handicapped are met. People with special problems should as far as possible be enabled to live in the community rather than in special residential care. In some cases the need is for specially designed or adapted housing, in others it is for help in obtaining ordinary housing.

(v) We must secure a reasonable degree of priority in access to public rented sector housing and home ownership for people in housing need who in the past have found themselves at the end of the queue. This includes for example some one-parent families, and middle-aged single people with modest incomes. They must not be left out in the cold.

---

*Public sector authorities charge rents related to the aggregate 'historic' construction costs or purchase price of all houses in their stock. Home owners' mortgage payments are linked to the price they originally paid for their house (which for any second-hand house is likely to be above the 'historic' cost paid by the first occupier of the house).

(vi) We must increase the scope for mobility in housing. It is essential, in a period of industrial change, that workers should be able to move house to change their job.

(vii) We must make it easier for people to obtain the tenure they want. More and more people would like to become home owners, or to enter the newer forms of tenure combining some of the advantages of home ownership and renting. We should not let our proper first concern for those who are badly housed lead us to overlook the reasonable housing ambitions of the community in general. As conditions ease, families should be able to look forward to widening opportunities for themselves, and for their children as they grow up.

(viii) We must safeguard the independence of tenants. All families have a right to expect a reasonable degree of freedom from interference in the way they use their homes.

2.17 The main elements of a policy designed to achieve the Government's housing objectives can be briefly summarised—at the risk of some over-simplification—in terms of the *supply* and *use* of housing.

2.18 The Government consider that to secure an adequate *supply* of housing of acceptable standards at a price within the reach of all families, housing investment must continue to be supported by general assistance. Public sector housing investment must be directed more selectively. This applies to the place, the timing and the type of investment. We can achieve this through housing strategies developed *locally* within the framework of a national housing policy. Such local housing strategies:

—will enable investment to be channelled in such a way that better progress is made in dealing with the needs of the most vulnerable households and the worst concentrations of bad housing, which are often found in the inner cities; and

—will reinforce the trend towards gradual renewal by a careful combination of renovation and rebuilding which reflects the needs and wishes of individuals.

2.19 The other side of the coin is the *use* of housing. This is closely bound up with tenure. People should have a reasonable chance of getting the kind of home they want. This will involve widening the way into home ownership; further development of 'intermediate' forms of tenure such as co-operative co-ownership and equity sharing; and the continuing provision of public rented sector housing for a wide cross-section of the population. We also need to develop a charter for tenants to strengthen their rights and freedoms.

2.20 Part II of the Green Paper (Chapters 3 to 5) gives a fuller description of the main features of the housing situation summarised in paragraphs 2.04 to 2.15 above—housing conditions, tenure, finance, and alternative approaches to pricing and assistance. Part III of the Green Paper discusses the Government's specific proposals for a national housing policy. The first chapter in Part III —Chapter 6—provides a general survey of the policy; the last chapter summarises the specific proposals.

Part II: Past and Present

CHAPTER 3

Housing Conditions and Tenure

3.01 Housing in England and Wales seems to be as good as in comparable countries, and there has been rapid and sustained progress since the war in improving housing conditions. Nevertheless, housing problems persist, and it is sometimes suggested that they may be getting worse.

3.02 To understand the present situation better, we need to look at:

—the size and quality of the housing stock in relation to the households to be accommodated;

—the effect of changes in housing tenure; and

—the relevant financial and economic trends.

The first two of these are considered in this chapter, and finance in the next chapter. There is additional statistical material in Annex B.

3.03 A word of caution is necessary about what follows. We are better informed than ever before, but we still do not have all the information we need. We now have up-to-date information on the condition of the housing stock from the House Condition Surveys 1976. But information on households and tenure is still based on the Census of 1971. Important changes have taken place since then but we can only make estimates of some of them. We need better and up-to-date information on such matters as the rate of household formation, changes in household composition, changes in the number of households sharing, vacant houses, and the composition and distribution of the private rented sector. We also need better information about differences between housing conditions in different areas. More up-to-date and comprehensive information will be obtained from a new National Housing Survey and a survey of vacant dwellings which will be launched later this year; and the Department of the Environment intend to establish a special Unit to analyse information about housing and to monitor progress.

THE HOUSING STOCK

3.04 For most of this century the dominant problem has been the sheer shortage of houses in relation to the number of households. For ten years in the first half of the century we were at war. In those years few houses were built, millions were badly maintained, and nearly a quarter of a million houses were destroyed. With a swiftly rising number of households the pressing need until very recently was for more houses of most kinds nearly everywhere. The problem of national housing shortage was aggravated by the inheritance from before the First World War of a large number of houses—about a third of the present housing stock in England and Wales was built before 1914—provided when standards were in many respects far below what are now acceptable.

9

3.05 Since the first major post-war assessment in the Census of 1951 housing conditions nationally have been transformed. There is no longer an absolute national shortage of houses. Whereas in 1951 there were about 750,000 more households than houses in England and Wales, by 1976 there were about 500,000 more houses than households (see Figure 1).

Figure 1: NATIONAL BALANCE (ENGLAND AND WALES) OF
DWELLINGS AND HOUSEHOLDS 1951 – 1976
(at five year intervals)

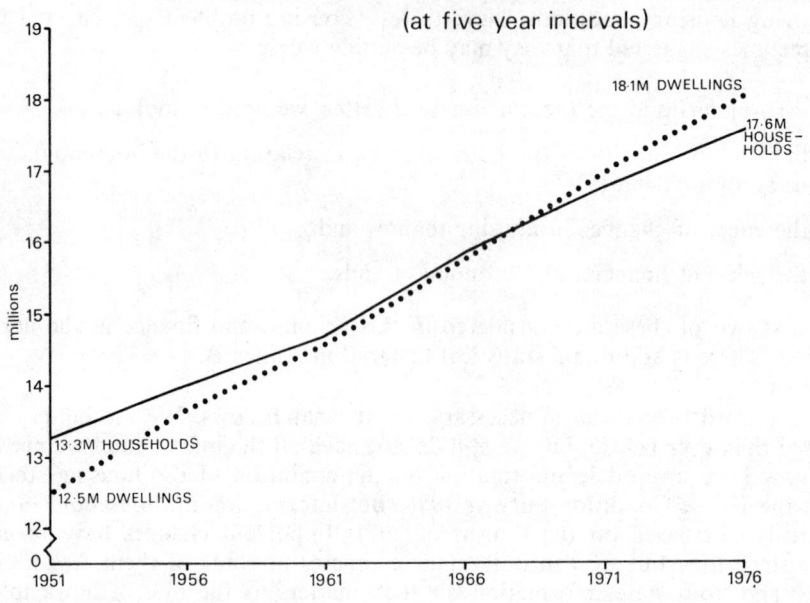

3.06 The fact that we now have more houses than households does not mean that all housing problems have been solved. About 300,000 houses in satisfactory condition were vacant in England and Wales in 1971; but we have to allow for a substantial number of houses which are bound to be vacant at any point in time for a variety of reasons—such as houses under repair or being prepared for incoming tenants or buyers; houses temporarily vacant while families are moving; and surplus houses in areas of declining population. Some houses are used as second homes. And we have to take account not only of the numbers of houses, but also of the housing conditions of the families living in them.

3.07 Housing conditions too have improved strikingly over the last 25 years. In 1951 there were about 10 million households in England and Wales living in unfit houses*, in substandard houses†, in overcrowded conditions‡, or sharing a house with other households. The comparable figure for 1976 was about 2·7 million (see Table 1).

---

*Houses statutorily unfit for human habitation.

†House not unfit but lacking one or more of the five basic amenities: a fixed bath in a bathroom; an inside WC; a wash basin; a sink; and a hot and cold water supply.

‡Density of occupation greater than 1·5 persons per room (this includes fewer households than would be counted as overcrowded by the widely used 'bedroom standard').

TABLE 1

ESTIMATE OF HOUSEHOLDS IN PHYSICALLY UNSATISFACTORY HOUSES, CROWDED OR SHARING

(England and Wales; thousands)

	1951	1976
Households in physically unsatisfactory houses:		
in unfit houses	} 7,500	700[a]
in substandard houses		950[a]
Households in overcrowded conditions	650	150
Households sharing (voluntarily and involuntarily)[b] ...	2,800	1,000
Totals[c]	9,700	2,700

(a) *Source:* House Condition Survey 1976.

(b) Includes 'concealed households' living as part of another household.

(c) Totals exclude overlaps and so are less than the sum of the items.

Over the last 5 years it is estimated that the number of unfit houses has been reduced by some 350,000—two-thirds by demolition and one-third by improvement*—some 900,000 sub-standard houses have been improved, overcrowding has fallen by a third, and sharing by a fifth.

3.08 These national statistics do not however tell the whole story about the remaining backlog of inadequate housing. They exclude houses which are technically neither unfit nor substandard, but are in serious disrepair. They take no account of families living in housing of good standard, but unsuited to their needs—for example families with small children in flats above ground level, and elderly or disabled people struggling with houses ill-adapted to their special problems. Broad-brush categorisations of unsatisfactory housing also fail to take account of the wide variations in the intensity of problems within the categories set out in paragraph 3.07:

—There are about 900,000 unfit houses in England and Wales, 700,000 of which are occupied. A large number will have to be replaced. But it may make better sense both financially and socially to give many of them a longer life by rehabilitation.

—'Substandard' houses cover a wide range of physical conditions. Many lack several amenities and will need a good deal of work and expenditure on rehabilitation. At the other extreme some lack only one amenity and could be brought up to standard by relatively simple and inexpensive works.

—There are even greater variations among 'sharing' households. These include not only families with children and childless couples but also middle-aged single people—unmarried, widowed or divorced—and young single people. Some of these households will be sharing involuntarily; some will be living in difficult domestic circumstances. But others may not regard their housing conditions as unsatisfactory.

*This is a net figure which takes account of additional houses becoming unfit.

—National figures conceal wide variations in the seriousness of local problems. We do not have consistent and up-to-date statistics for all the individual local authorities, but we know that in some areas there is virtually no deficit of decent housing, while other areas have intense concentrations of bad housing, often associated with other social problems, which contribute to a downward spiral of neglect and decay. Poor housing is one of the most obvious symptoms of the collective deprivation suffered by people living in the failing areas of many major cities, as is well illustrated in the recently published reports of the Inner Area Studies of London, Liverpool and Birmingham. In Wales there are 100,000 houses unfit, of which 80,000 are occupied—about 8 per cent of the total Welsh housing stock.

3.09 It is clear therefore that we over-simplify the problem if we speak of 'housing need' as an absolute condition which can be measured precisely. The range and degree of need is very wide and difficult to gauge; but there is without doubt a substantial number of households who are still very inadequately housed. This clearly applies to people living in unfit houses and in overcrowded conditions. It also applies to many of the households living in substandard houses and some of those who are sharing. Probably at least 1·8 million households in England and Wales—more than one in ten—are living in circumstances which are just not acceptable by contemporary standards. This is the hard core of housing need; and it shades into housing conditions which though less unsatisfactory are not good enough and ought to be improved.

3.10 We have to make provision for working through this backlog of inadequate housing conditions. We have to allow for replacement of some of the houses which will become unfit—between 1971 and 1976 houses became unfit at a rate of 50,000–70,000 a year—and of fit houses which are unavoidably demolished. We also have to provide for the growth in household numbers.

3.11 The projected average rate of net new household formation* in England and Wales in the next ten years is 135,000 a year. This arises partly from growth in the proportion of the population of marriageable age, and more importantly from an increase in the number of people—particularly the elderly—living as one-person households. The projection is based on past trends, but the future rate of net household formation will of course depend in part on the supply of houses and their prices or rents.

3.12 A substantial level of new housebuilding will be necessary to cope with the increase in the numbers of households, to meet the needs of some households who are currently sharing involuntarily or who are overcrowded, and to replace houses which have to be demolished. But much can be done by rehabilitation, conversion and repair of existing houses and by better use of the existing stock.

---

*The rate at which the formation of new households is expected to exceed the dissolution of existing households.

HOUSING TENURE

3.13 The ability to get a decent home depends not only on the supply of housing, but on the factors, different in each tenure, which determine access to housing.

3.14 There is a good deal of movement into and between the three main tenures each year. Detailed estimates for Great Britain have been made for 1971.*

—*Owner-occupied sector.* 460,000 households entered the sector; 410,000 households moved within the sector; 70,000 moved to other tenures; and 170,000 households within the sector were dissolved on death, other household dissolution, or emigration.

—*Local authority and new town tenancies.* 325,000 households came in; 230,000 moved within the sector; 100,000 moved to other tenures; and 90,000 households within the sector were dissolved.

—*Private rented sector.* 440,000 households came in (including single people living alone in a rented room); 300,000 moved from one tenancy to another; 390,000 moved to other tenures; and 185,000 households were dissolved.

In all, after eliminating double counting, about 2·1 million households moved, including new households moving into their first home—about one household in nine in Great Britain.

3.15 Entry into or moves within the owner-occupied sector are affected by the judgement of lenders on the credit-worthiness of the applicant and on whether the house in question is adequate security for a loan. Entry into or moves within the public rented sector depend primarily on a socially determined view of housing need. The position is complicated by the fact that judgements made on individual applications can vary from local authority to local authority and building society to building society. Sometimes there is good reason for variations in practice—for example, a local authority in an area where there is no significant shortage of good housing can take a more lenient view of housing need than an authority still confronted with pressing housing problems; and some building societies specialise in lending on particular types of houses. But sometimes variations in practice reflect traditional attitudes which are difficult for the applicant to understand and readily accept as reasonable. Those who cannot buy a house or obtain a public rented sector house have to look to the private rented sector for accommodation.

3.16 One of the major social changes of our time has been the shift in the structure of housing tenure—the rise of home ownership and public sector renting, and the decline of private renting. At the end of the First World War probably 90 per cent of the housing stock was rented privately, and virtually the whole of the remainder was owner-occupied. Now, in England and Wales about 55 per cent of houses are owner-occupied, 30 per cent are in the public sector, and only 15 per cent are rented privately (see Figure 2).

---

*See Technical Volume, Chapters 2 and 3.

Figure 2 : HOUSING TENURE IN 1951, 1971, AND 1976
(ENGLAND AND WALES)

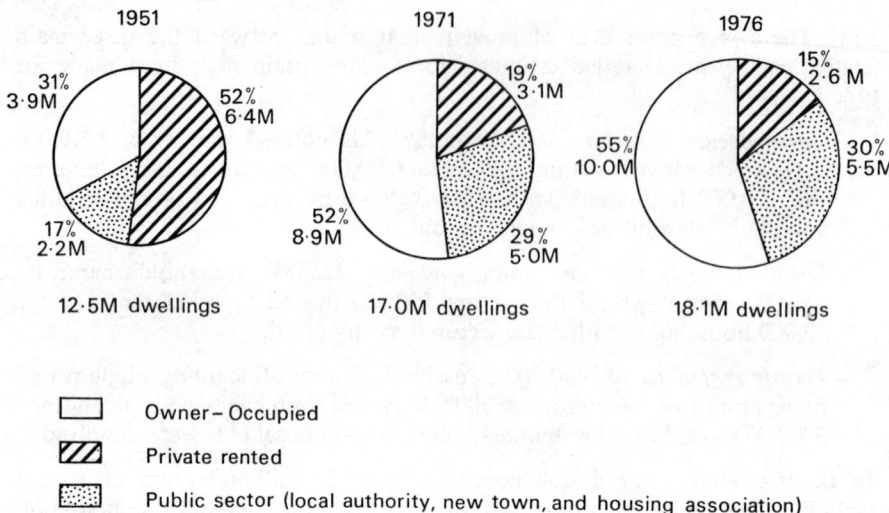

1951

31%
3·9M
52%
6·4M
17%
2·2M

12·5M dwellings

1971

19%
3·1M
52%
8·9M
29%
5·0M

17·0M dwellings

1976

15%
2·6 M
55%
10·0M
30%
5·5M

18·1M dwellings

☐ Owner – Occupied

▨ Private rented

▦ Public sector (local authority, new town, and housing association)

3.17 The reasons for the changes in the size of the three tenures are complex. There have been powerful social and financial influences operating both on the demand for houses in different tenures and on the supply.

3.18 Non-financial considerations may have played a large part in the growth of the owner-occupied and public rented sectors. People are attracted to home ownership by the opportunity for personal freedom and independence. Local authorities have been extending their range to provide not only for families with children, but also for groups with special needs such as frail elderly people or the physically disabled. Moreover many tenants prefer a socially accountable public landlord to a private landlord. But in addition, general assistance has made these tenures more attractive to many households than renting from a private landlord. Even in the absence of rent control and regulation, competition from the sectors aided by general assistance would have made it difficult for landlords to get a commercially attractive return on new houses and flats. These and other factors often make sale for home ownership more attractive to landlords, although many continue to relet.

3.19 It is difficult to envisage a *reversal* of the contraction of the private rented sector. But there are about 7 million people still living in private rented accommodation, and so the private rented sector will be of great importance for many years to come. This is why the Government are carrying out the Review of the Rent Acts.

3.20 We should be in a position to reach conclusions on the Review of the Rent Acts later this year. But it is already clear that the continuing contraction of the private rented sector can cause problems for some people who for one reason or another come at the end of the queue for home ownership or public sector renting. This is particularly evident in the inner cities, where private lettings often make up an important part of the housing stock. Such people may be:

—*mobile workers*—including immigrant families—newly arrived in the locality who may not be able to get a mortgage;

—*one-parent families*, many of whom face similar difficulties as a result of moving home after marital breakup and staying temporarily with relatives;

—*married couples without children*, who may face a long period of saving before they can hope to afford home ownership;

—*single people with modest incomes* who cannot afford to buy. There has been a rapid increase in the number of one person households in all age groups since 1961—86 per cent as against 8 per cent for multi-person households. Some of these households are widows and widowers in satisfactory housing. Many of the rest may have no special problem in obtaining accommodation. But some may be faced with acute problems because of the continuing contraction of the private rented sector.

CHAPTER 4

Housing Finance

4.01 Total private and public investment* in housing in the United Kingdom†
grew for most of the post-war period, both in absolute terms and as a proportion
of the Gross Domestic Product. At the start of the nineteen seventies it was
only about £3,900m compared with nearly £4,400m in 1968/69; but it rose to
£4,800m in 1972/73 and to £5,600m in 1973/74, and stayed within 5% of this level
in 1974/75 and in 1975/76 (1976/77 prices). But since the early nineteen seventies
there has been a disconcerting shift in the pattern of expenditure. General
assistance and rent rebates have risen at a much faster rate than investment—
122 per cent between 1969/70 and 1975/76 as opposed to 35 per cent for invest-
m'ent (see Figure 3). Nevertheless, despite the increase in general assistance,
net mortgage payments and rents rose rapidly.

INVESTMENT, SUBSIDY, AND HOUSEHOLDERS' PAYMENTS

4.02 The cost of housing depends on the price of land and the capital cost of
new building and improvement, both of which are influenced by demand.
Demand for housing is affected by income levels, the cost of borrowing, and
the net costs which householders have to meet themselves in the form of rents
or mortgage payments net of tax relief. The picture is further complicated
because local authorities' decisions on housing investment depend on social as
well as financial factors; and effective demand for home ownership can be
limited by the availability of mortgage funds. But although there is no straight-
forward relationship between costs, incomes, assistance and investment, higher
net costs to householders will tend to reduce the demand for new and improved
houses, and so in turn lead to lower investment, and *vice versa*.

4.03 The annual borrowing costs on a house depend primarily on the 'historic'
cost—the price paid by the current owner, whether a home owner or a local
authority—and on the interest rate. The average capital debt was about £4,000
for each mortgaged house at the end of 1976, and between £2,500 and £3,000
for each public sector house at the end of 1975/76. Because of the large amount
of debt, housing costs are crucially affected by interest rates. Interest charges
make up about three-fifths of housing costs.

4.04 The current forms of general assistance meet a proportion of borrowing
costs. If borrowing costs rise—either because land prices and building costs
or house prices go up, or because of increases in interest rates—then there is an
increase in both householders' net payments and general assistance. The effects
are different for new investment and the outstanding debt on existing houses,
since the latter is affected only by interest rate increases.

4.05 Increases in prices and interest rates affect householders' payments
differently in the two main sectors because of fundamental differences in their
financial arrangements.

---

*Investment includes, in the public sector, capital expenditure on new building (including
land), acquisition, and improvement of houses in Housing Revenue Accounts; and in the
private sector, expenditure by home owners on the purchase of new homes, and grant-aided
improvements.

†Separate England and Wales figures for investment and assistance in the owner-occupied
sector are not available. Consequently, although England and Wales figures are used where
the public sector is discussed alone in this chapter, the figures for aggregate investment and
assistance in both main sectors, or for investment, assistance, or net payments in the owner-
occupied sector, are UK-based.

Figure 3: HOUSING INVESTMENT AND ASSISTANCE
1969/70–1975/76 *
(United Kingdom; £M at 1976 – 77 prices)

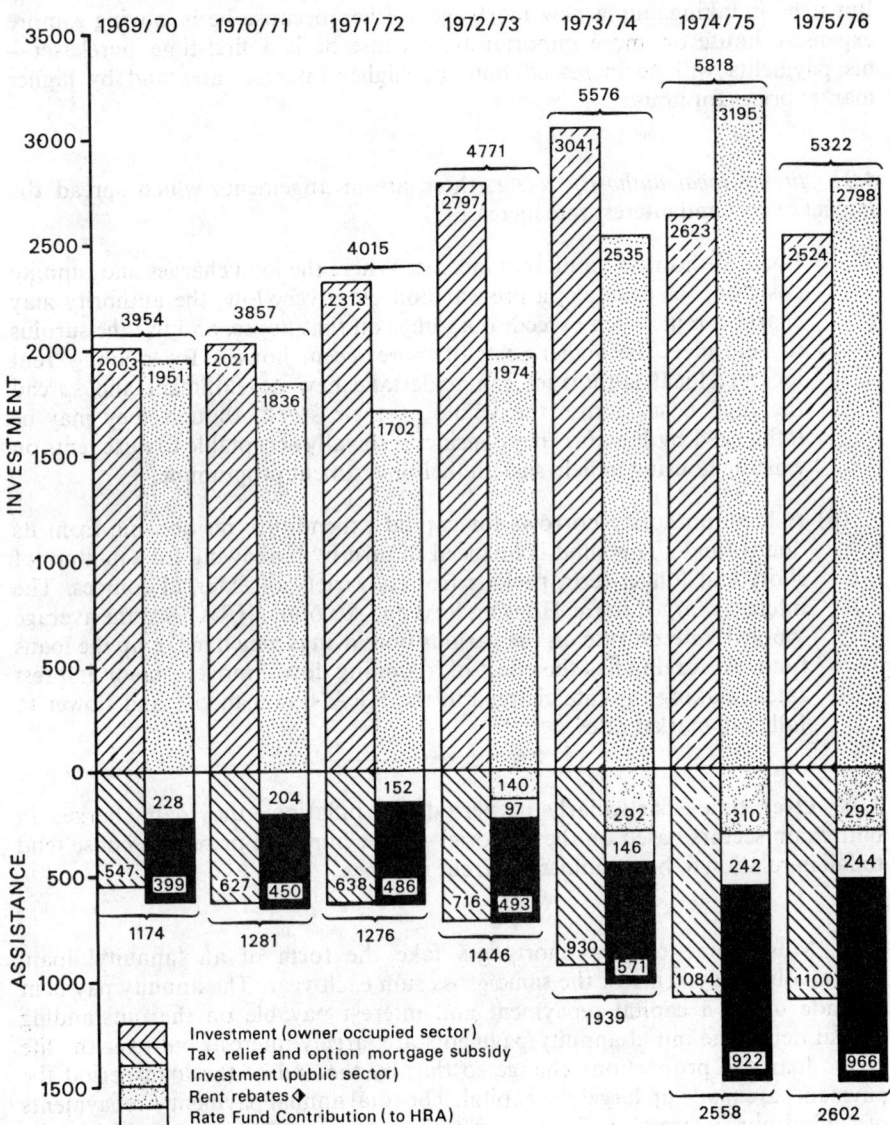

* The categories of housing investment included in this diagram are those listed in the footnote to paragraph 4.01. The categories of assistance exclude rent allowances.

◆ Rent rebates for 1971/72 and earlier years are included with rate fund contributions and subsidy

4.06 *In the owner-occupied sector* the effect depends upon the position of the individual householder—whether he owns his house outright, has a mortgage outstanding, or is just becoming a home owner. If he owns his house outright he will be unaffected. If he still has a mortgage, his costs will rise with increases in interest rates by an amount depending on how large a loan he has outstanding. But if he is taking out a new mortgage—either because he is buying a more expensive house or, more importantly, because he is a first-time purchaser— his payments will be increased both by higher interest rates and by higher market prices for houses.

4.07 *In the local authority sector*, there are arrangements which spread the impact of cost and interest rate increases;

(i) Local authorities 'pool' rent income. Where the loan charges and running costs on, for example, a pre-war house are very low, the authority may charge a rent which exceeds outgoings on that house, and use the surplus to help meet the higher costs of more recent houses. By 'pooling' rent income, local authorities can undertake new development and spread the high costs across the whole of their stock, though they may be influenced by how far they consider it socially acceptable to raise rents on existing housing to help sustain their investment programme.

(ii) A local authority borrows for capital expenditure on housing from its 'loans fund'. This fund is financed in turn by borrowing for a mixture of short and longer-term periods from a variety of external sources. The interest charged to the Housing Revenue Account (HRA) is at the average 'pooled' interest rate on the various borrowings which make up the loans fund. Averaging has the effect of 'damping down' movements in interest rates, making the rate charged to the HRA slower to rise and slower to fall than market rates.

4.08 Over time—particularly in periods of inflation—the loan charges in both main sectors based on the 'historic' cost or purchase price of a house tend to fall in relation to householders' current incomes.

4.09 Most home owners' mortgages take the form of an 'annuity' loan. This involves payments of the same gross sum each year. The annuity payment is made up of a capital repayment and interest payable on the outstanding capital debt. The initial annuity payments are largely interest, but over the life of the loan the proportions change so that by the end of the loan period the payments are made up largely of capital. The total annual payment—repayments of capital plus interest—is fixed when the mortgage is taken out and normally alters subsequently only if the interest rate changes. If incomes rise in money terms and interest rates do not increase, the burden of payments reduces in *real* terms over the years. When interest rates are high and money incomes are rising swiftly, initial payments are higher and a large proportion of the total cost of the mortgage in real terms is concentrated in the early years. This is known as 'front loading' (see Figure 4).

18

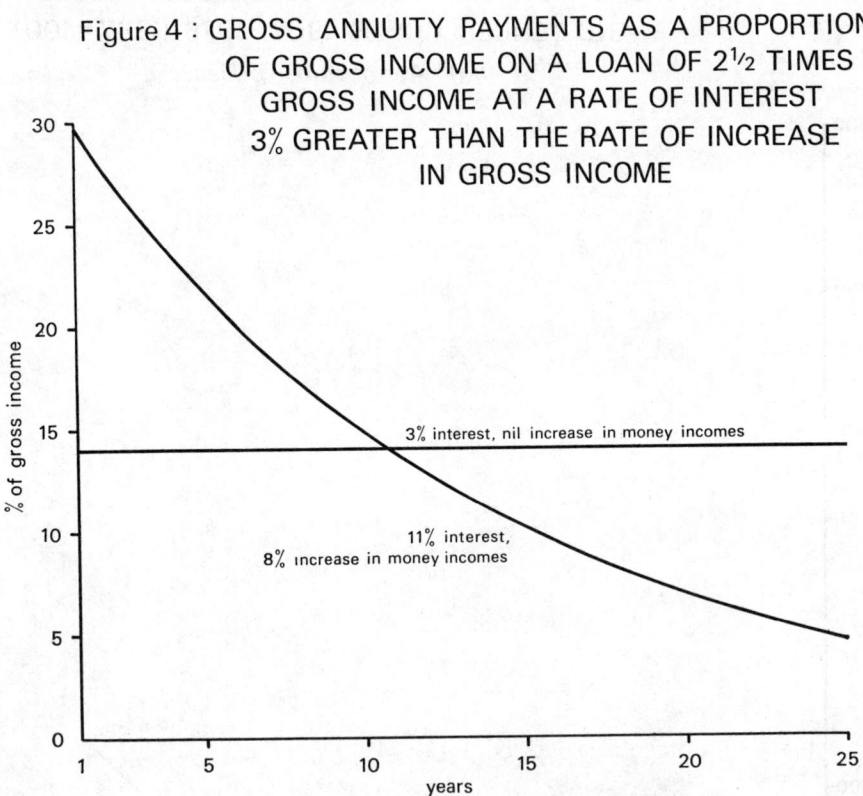

Figure 4 : GROSS ANNUITY PAYMENTS AS A PROPORTION
OF GROSS INCOME ON A LOAN OF 2½ TIMES
GROSS INCOME AT A RATE OF INTEREST
3% GREATER THAN THE RATE OF INCREASE
IN GROSS INCOME

4.10   The pattern is similar for a local authority's loan charges on its existing housing. There are differences due for example to refinancing of existing debt. But except in periods of rapidly rising interest rates the loan charges arising from existing housing tend to fall over time in relation to tenants' incomes— though rent payments may continue to rise, chiefly as a result of rent pooling to help meet the higher costs of additional new investment.

COST INCREASES IN THE NINETEEN SEVENTIES

4.11   Interest rates and the rate of inflation were much lower in the nineteen fifties and nineteen sixties than in recent years. Consequently 'front loading' was of relatively little significance. Housing costs, earnings, net payments for housing, and housing assistance moved ahead broadly in step until about the middle nineteen sixties, and the amount of general assistance needed to maintain a given relationship between the net annual cost of new housing and the general level of incomes was much less than in recent years. By the mid-nineteen sixties the rise in the initial annual costs of new houses was enough to cause concern. One result was a shift in the Housing Subsidies Act 1967 from a subsidy in the traditional form of a fixed annual sum per house to a percentage subsidy related to capital costs and interest rates. And the early nineteen seventies witnessed a marked change.

19

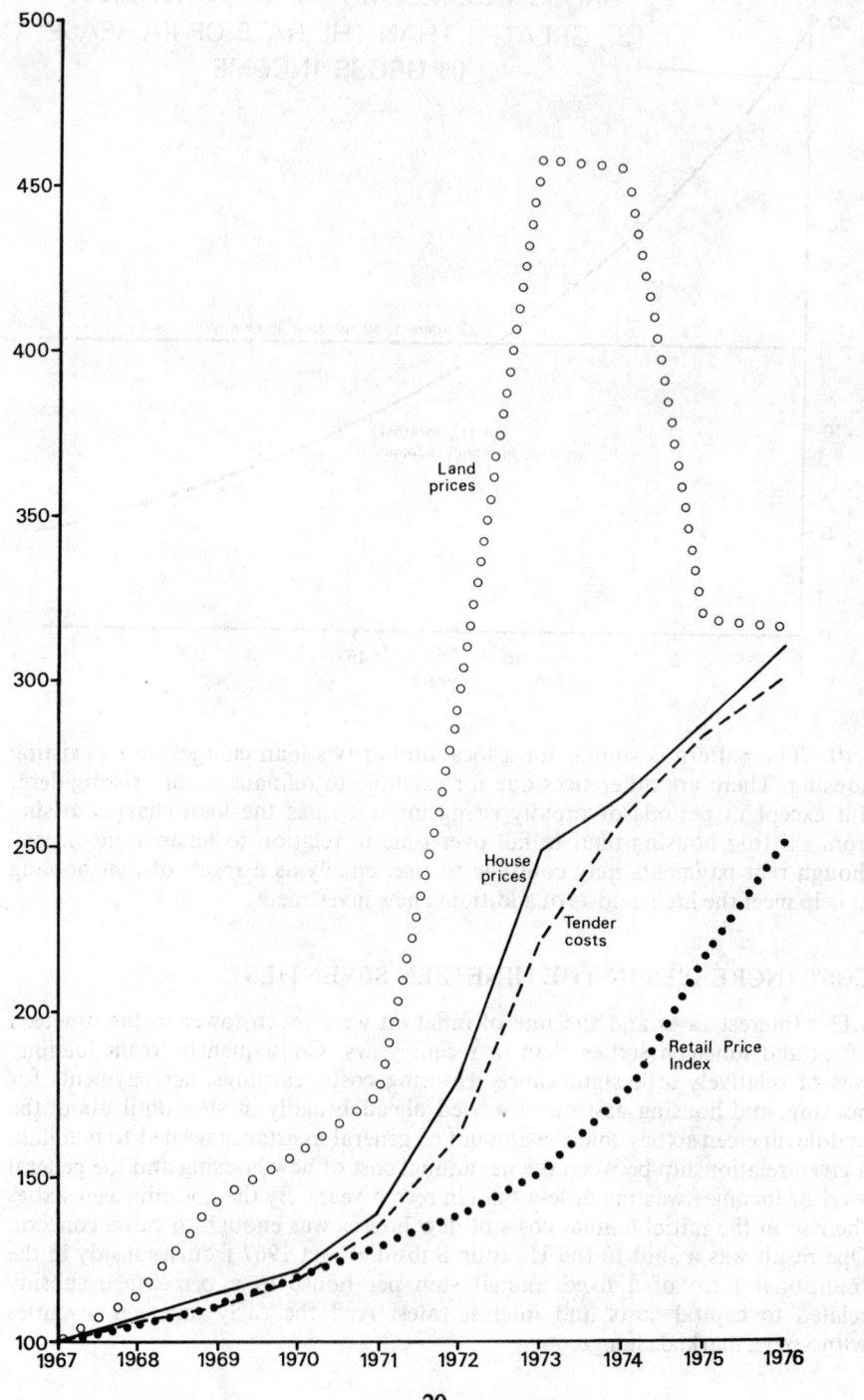

Figure 5: INDICES OF LAND PRICES, HOUSE PRICES
AND TENDER COSTS 1967–1976 (1967=100)

(a) At outturn prices

Land
prices

House
prices

Tender
costs

Retail Price
Index

(b) In real terms (relative to RPI)

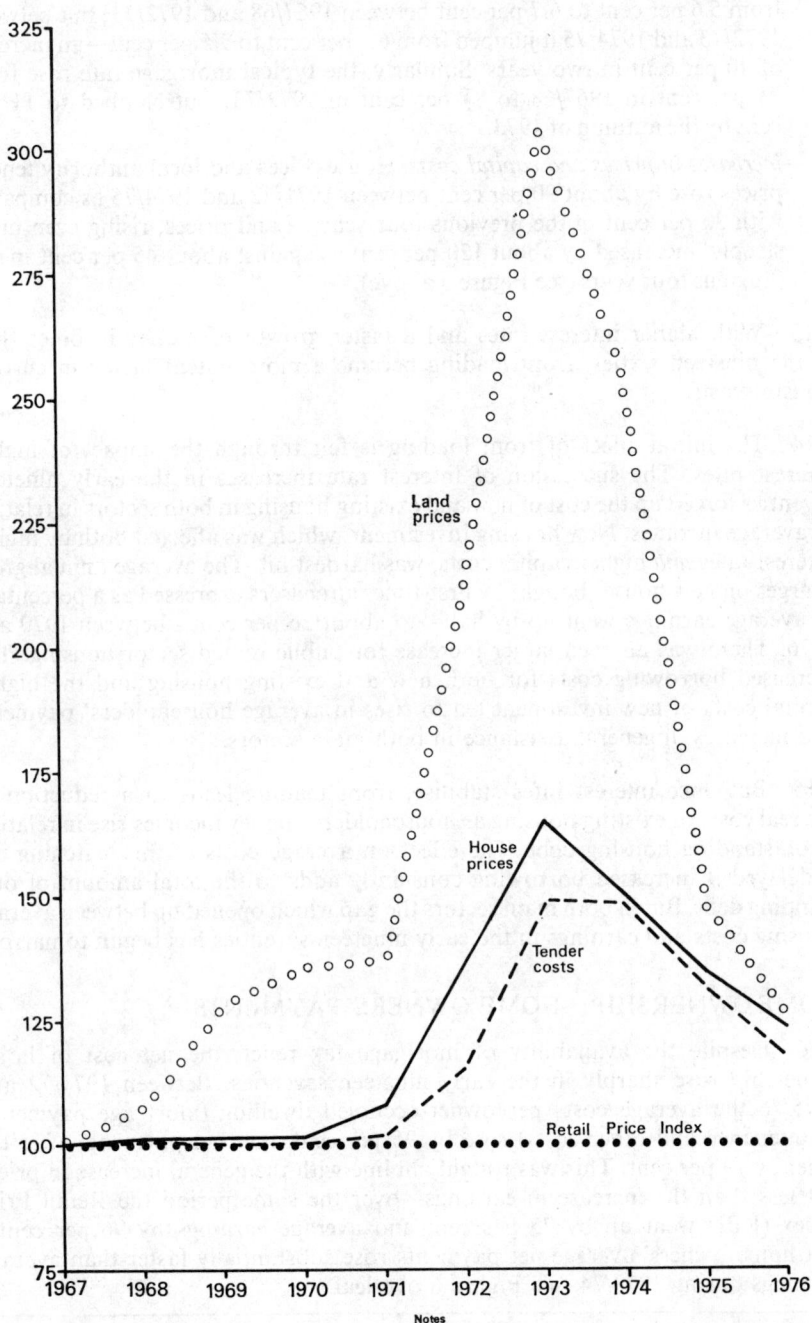

Land prices

House prices

Tender costs

Retail Price Index

325
300
275
250
225
200
175
150
125
100
75

1967 1968 1969 1970 1971 1972 1973 1974 1975 1976

Notes

These graphs represent: (a) The price per plot of building land for private owners, England and Wales.- (b) The price of new houses, UK. (c) The Price Index for Local Authority housebuilding, England and Wales.

21

4.12 In the early nineteen seventies there were unprecedented increases in interest rates and capital costs:

—*rises in interest rates.* The average local authority 'pool' rate rose only from 5.6 per cent to 6.7 per cent between 1967/68 and 1972/73; but between 1972/73 and 1974/75 it jumped from 6.7 per cent to 9.5 per cent—an increase of 40 per cent in two years. Similarly, the typical mortgage rate rose from $7\frac{1}{8}$ per cent in 1967/68 to $8\frac{1}{2}$ per cent in 1972/73; but climbed to 11 per cent by the autumn of 1973.

—*increases in prices and capital costs.* House prices and local authority tender prices rose by about 90 per cent between 1971/72 and 1974/75 as compared with 30 per cent in the previous four years. Land prices, rising even more steeply, increased by about 120 per cent as against about 45 per cent in the previous four years (see Figure 5 above).

4.13 With higher interest rates and a faster growth of money incomes than in the nineteen sixties, front loading became a more potent factor in current housing costs.

4.14 The initial effect of front loading is felt through the impact of higher interest rates. The succession of interest rate increases in the early nineteen seventies forced up the cost of new and existing housing in both sectors in relation to average incomes. New housing investment, which was affected both by higher interest rates *and* higher capital costs, was hardest hit. The average annual gross charges on new houses bought by first-time purchasers expressed as a percentage of average earnings went up by half—to about 36 per cent—between 1970 and 1976. There was an even larger increase for public rented sector housing. The increased borrowing costs for both new and existing housing and the higher capital costs of new investment led to rises in average householders' payments and increases in general assistance in both main sectors.

4.15 But once interest rates stabilise, front loading leads to a reduction in the real costs of existing housing as householders' money incomes rise in relation to outstanding housing debt. The effect on average costs of this 'catching up' is delayed if increased borrowing constantly adds to the total amount of outstanding debt. But in both main sectors the gap which opened up between average housing costs and earnings in the early nineteen seventies has begun to narrow.

HOME OWNERSHIP: HOME OWNERS' PAYMENTS

4.16 Despite the availability of mortgage tax relief, the net cost of home ownership rose sharply in the early nineteen seventies. Between 1971/72 and 1975/76 the average costs per owner-occupied dwelling (mortgage payments, maintenance and other costs) rose by 95 per cent, and net payments after tax relief by 79 per cent. This was roughly in line with the general increase in prices but less than the increase in earnings—over the same period the Retail Price Index (RPI) went up by 75 per cent and average earnings by 96 per cent*. But home owners' average net payments rose substantially faster than average earnings during 1973/74 (see Figure 6 overleaf).

---

*Before tax. The rate of increase net of tax was smaller, by an amount which varied with the tax position of the householder.

4.17 The amount of mortgage tax relief—which in the normal case meets about one-third of gross mortgage interest—grew sharply both because of the rise in house prices and interest rates, and because of the growth in home ownership. It increased from £638m in 1971/72 to £1,100m in 1975/76 (UK, 1976/77 prices). Other less important factors were the rise in the basic rate of tax from 30 per cent in 1973/74 to 33 per cent in 1974/75 and 35 per cent in 1975/76 which increased the amount of tax relief; and on the other hand the introduction in 1974/75 of the limitation on borrowing eligible for tax relief to £25,000 on the owner's principal residence. The increase in mortgage tax relief meant that the proportion of total gross annual outgoings met by home owners fell from about 84 per cent in 1971/72 to 79 per cent in 1975/76.

4.18 With higher prices and interest rates, first-time home buyers commonly had to set aside more than 20 per cent of post-tax income to meet initial mortgage payments. Nevertheless, the strong preference for home ownership was evident in the fact that in general the demand for mortgages continued to exceed the supply.

HOME OWNERSHIP: INVESTMENT

4.19 The level of housing investment in the owner-occupied sector rose in the early nineteen seventies to about £3,000m in 1973/74 (UK, 1967/77 prices). It fell subsequently not so much because of any sustained reduction in demand —despite increases in house prices and interest rates—but because of a sharp drop in the supply of mortgage funds at the end of 1973 and the beginning of 1974.

4.20 Building societies' mortgage lending, and hence the receipts from investors needed to finance it, have grown rapidly and will continue to do so. The past growth is illustrated in Figure 7. The growth comes in part from the continuing net additions to the owner-occupied stock from new building and purchases of formerly rented houses. But the gross demand for mortgage funds will also reflect the extent to which houses formerly owned outright—for example by elderly home owners—are sold to new purchasers financing the sale by mortgages; and the increasing number of second hand houses changing hands as the owner-occupied housing stock grows (although to a considerable extent such purchases can be financed out of capital receipts from sales). Furthermore, the amount of funds needed for these purposes will continue to be affected for some years by the exceptional increase in house prices between 1971 and 1974, as mortgages of amounts that reflect today's house prices replace mortgages taken out either before or at the beginning of the surge in house prices.

4.21 But building societies' receipts from investors—especially those in larger amounts such as £2,000 and upwards—have proved very sensitive to changes in the balance between the interest rate offered by societies and those offered by their competitors. These competing rates, perhaps especially those offered by banks for large deposits, have been subject in the nineteen seventies to changes of as much as 4 per cent in three months—more severe than anything seen in the nineteen fifties and nineteen sixties. Consequently, building societies'

23

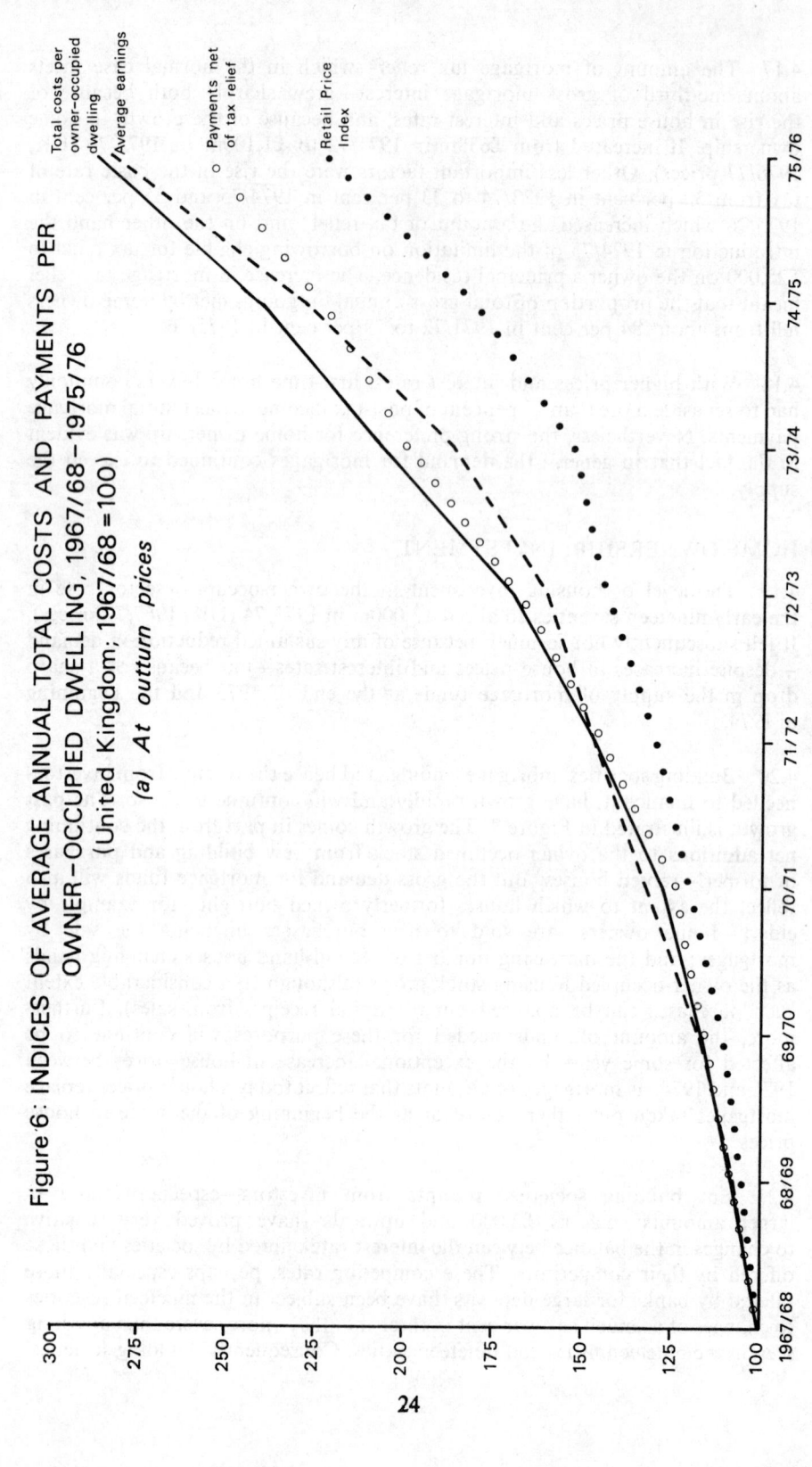

Figure 6: INDICES OF AVERAGE ANNUAL TOTAL COSTS AND PAYMENTS PER OWNER-OCCUPIED DWELLING, 1967/68–1975/76

(United Kingdom; 1967/68 = 100)

(a) At outturn prices

Total costs per owner-occupied dwelling

Average earnings

○ Payments net of tax relief

• Retail Price Index

(b) In real terms (relative to RPI)

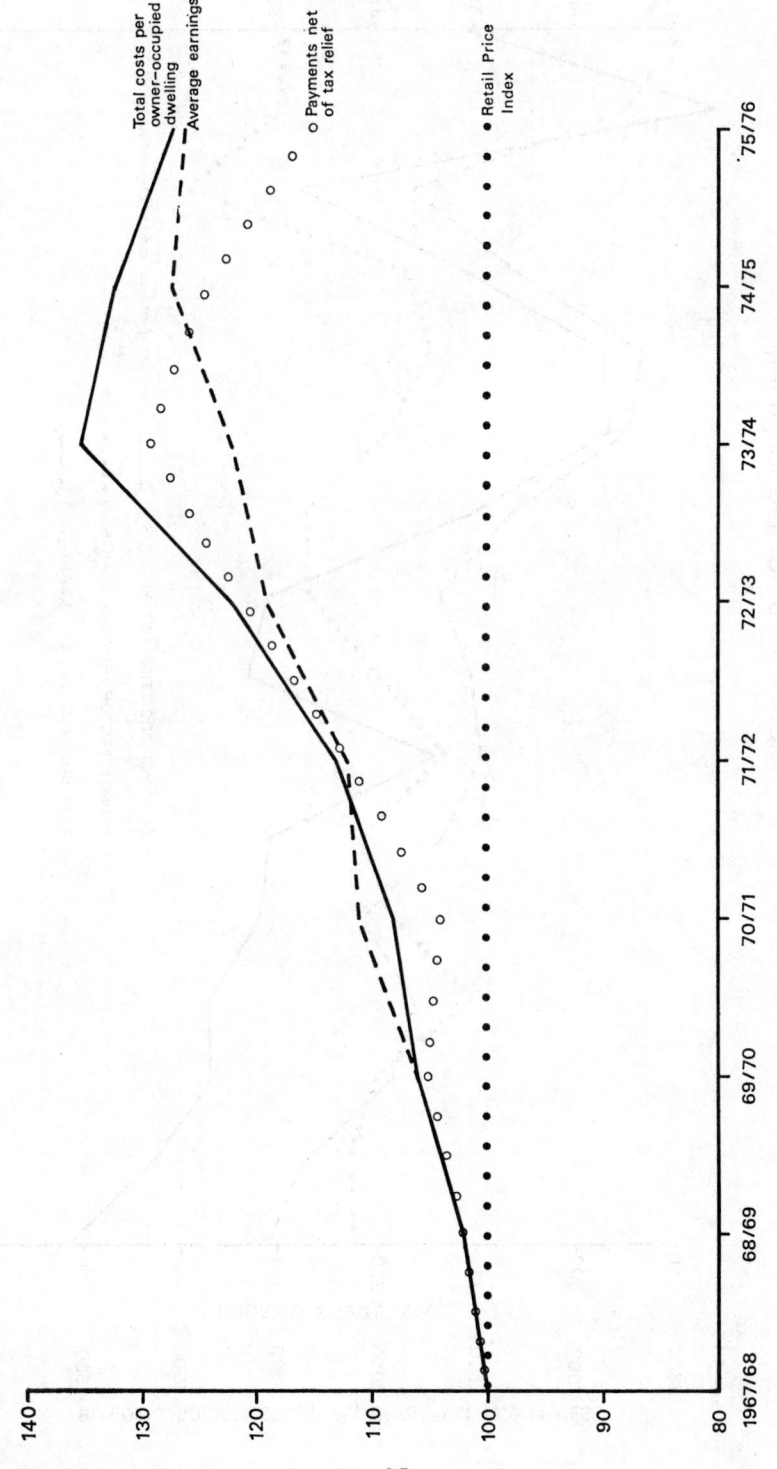

Total costs per
owner—occupied
dwelling
Average earnings

o Payments net
of tax relief

• Retail Price
Index

Notes (a) 'Total costs' include mortgage payments, repair and transaction costs and are calculated by reference to all owner occupied dwellings including those free of mortgage
(b) 'Average earnings' are derived from the Department of Employment's monthly index of average pre-tax earnings of all employees, manual and non-manual.

25

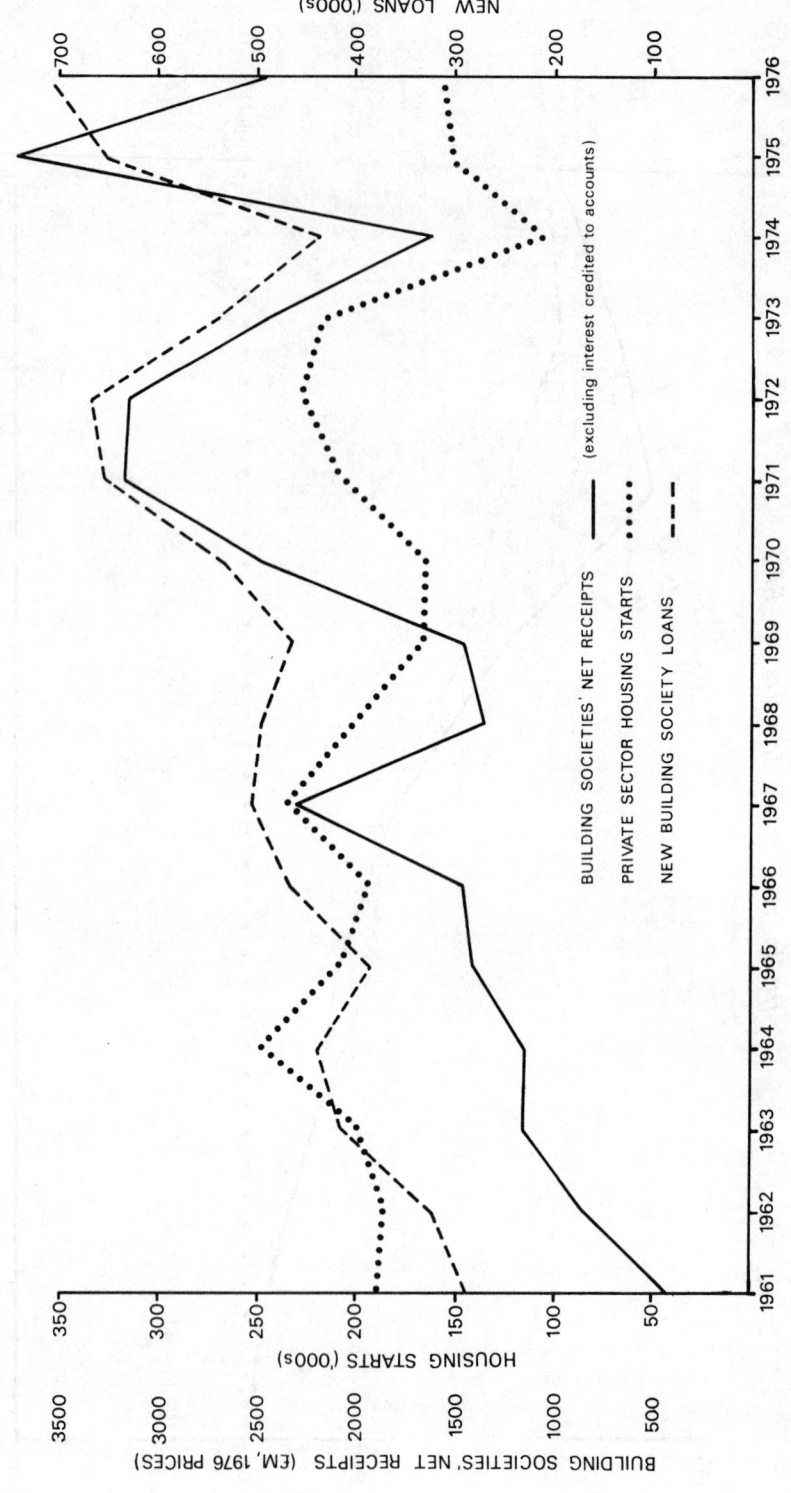

Figure 7 : BUILDING SOCIETIES' NET RECEIPTS, MORTGAGE LENDING AND HOUSING STARTS 1961—1976 (United Kingdom)

net inflows have fluctuated by large amounts, for example from an average of £366m a month in February-March 1976 to £25m a month in November-December, and back to £493m in April-May 1977.

4.22 Before the present stabilisation arrangements—discussed in Chapter 7—were introduced, the large variations in building society receipts resulted in alternating mortgage 'feasts and famines' (see Figure 7). When interest rates fell, money poured into building societies. The lending on mortgage of this influx of funds contributed to the surge in house prices in 1971–73. The period of severe mortgage rationing in 1973-74—which ended more quickly than it would otherwise have done after the Government's provision of £500m in short term loans—led to a halving within a year of the number of new houses started for sale for home ownership. The number of private sector housing starts in England and Wales fell from about 200,000 in 1973 to about 96,000 in 1974; there was then some recovery and a steadier level of housebuilding—about 137,000 houses were started in 1975 and 138,000 in 1976.

PUBLIC RENTED SECTOR: RENTS

4.23 The increase in capital costs and interest rates—together with higher costs of management and maintenance—resulted in an increase in local authority HRA costs in England and Wales averaging 116 per cent per dwelling between 1971/72 and 1975/76. Over the same period unrebated rents went up by 76 per cent. This was about the same as the RPI (75 per cent) but less than average earnings (96 per cent). Rebated rents went up by 40 per cent (Figure 8).

4.24 Despite rent increases, the proportion of sharply rising total HRA costs met by unrebated rents fell from 77 per cent in 1972/73 to 57 per cent in 1975/76. Subsidies and rate fund contributions bridged the gap: in the most difficult years, rent increases covered only one quarter of the cost increases. Exchequer general subsidies rose automatically as costs increased. There was also a change in the system of subsidies, when the system set up under the Housing Finance Act 1972 was replaced by the interim arrangements in the Housing Rents and Subsidies Act 1975. This Act consolidated previously existing HRA subsidies under the 1972 Act at the level they had reached in 1974/75. It provided new elements of subsidy related to the costs of new investment and to increases in the cost of servicing 'old' debt, together with special additional subsidies for the higher cost areas. In addition, extra subsidies were paid to enable rents to be held down as part of counter-inflationary policy in 1974/75 and 1975/76. Exchequer general subsidies rose from £381m in 1971/72 to £776m in 1975/76. General Rate Fund contributions to HRAs rose from £78m in 1971/72 to £199m in 1975/76 (England and Wales, 1976/77 prices).

4.25 Rent rebate schemes, which were made mandatory in 1972, protect lower-income tenants from the full impact of rent increases. A tenant with a rebate would normally pay about 40 per cent of a rent increase. Currently 75 per cent of the cost of rebates is met by the Exchequer and the remainder from the authority's General Rate Fund. The sum spent on rent rebates rose from about £35m in 1971/72 to £259m in 1975/76 (England and Wales, 1976/77 prices). Allowing for rebates the proportion of HRA costs met by rents in 1975/76 was 45 per cent.

27

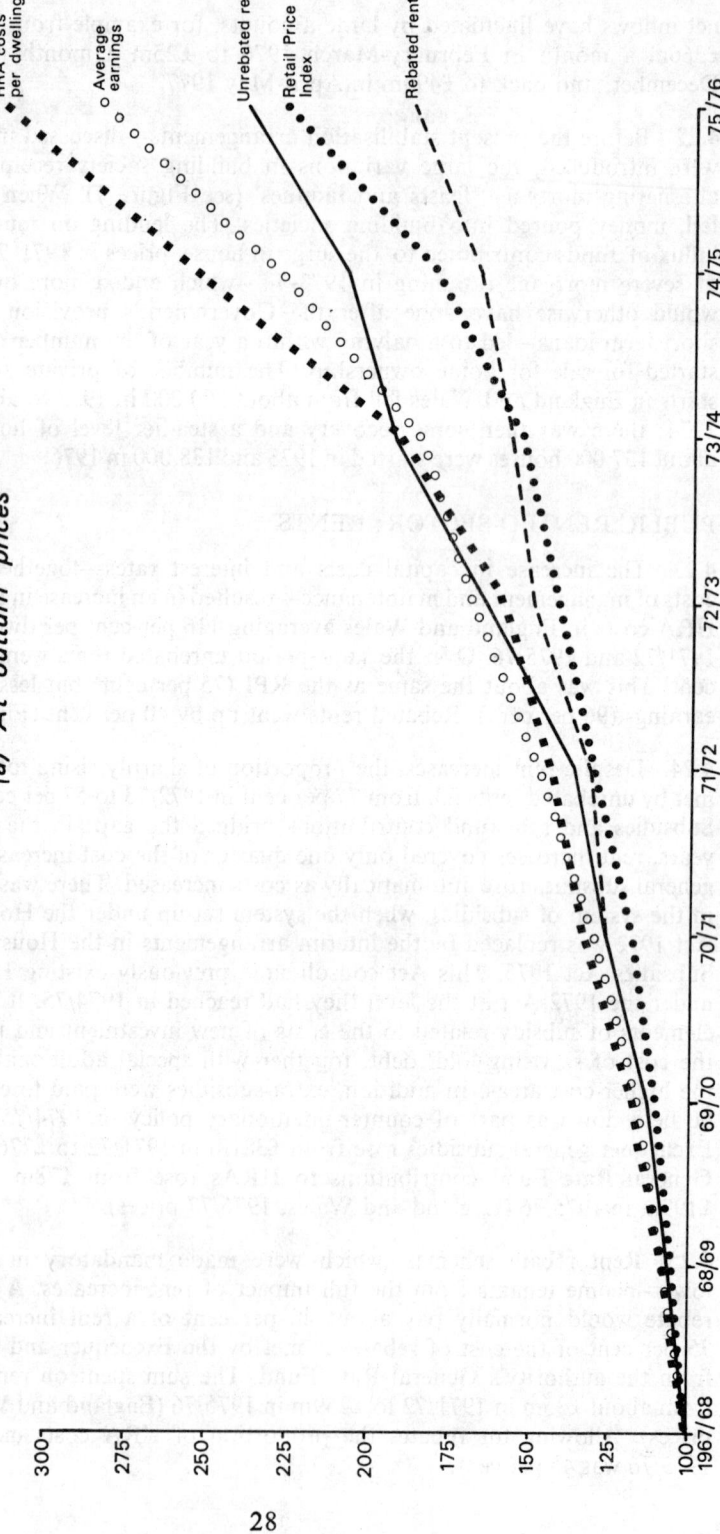

Figure 8: INDICES OF AVERAGE HOUSING REVENUE ACCOUNT COSTS AND LOCAL AUTHORITY RENTS PER DWELLING, 1967/68–1975/76 (ENGLAND AND WALES; 1967/68=100)

(a) At outturn prices

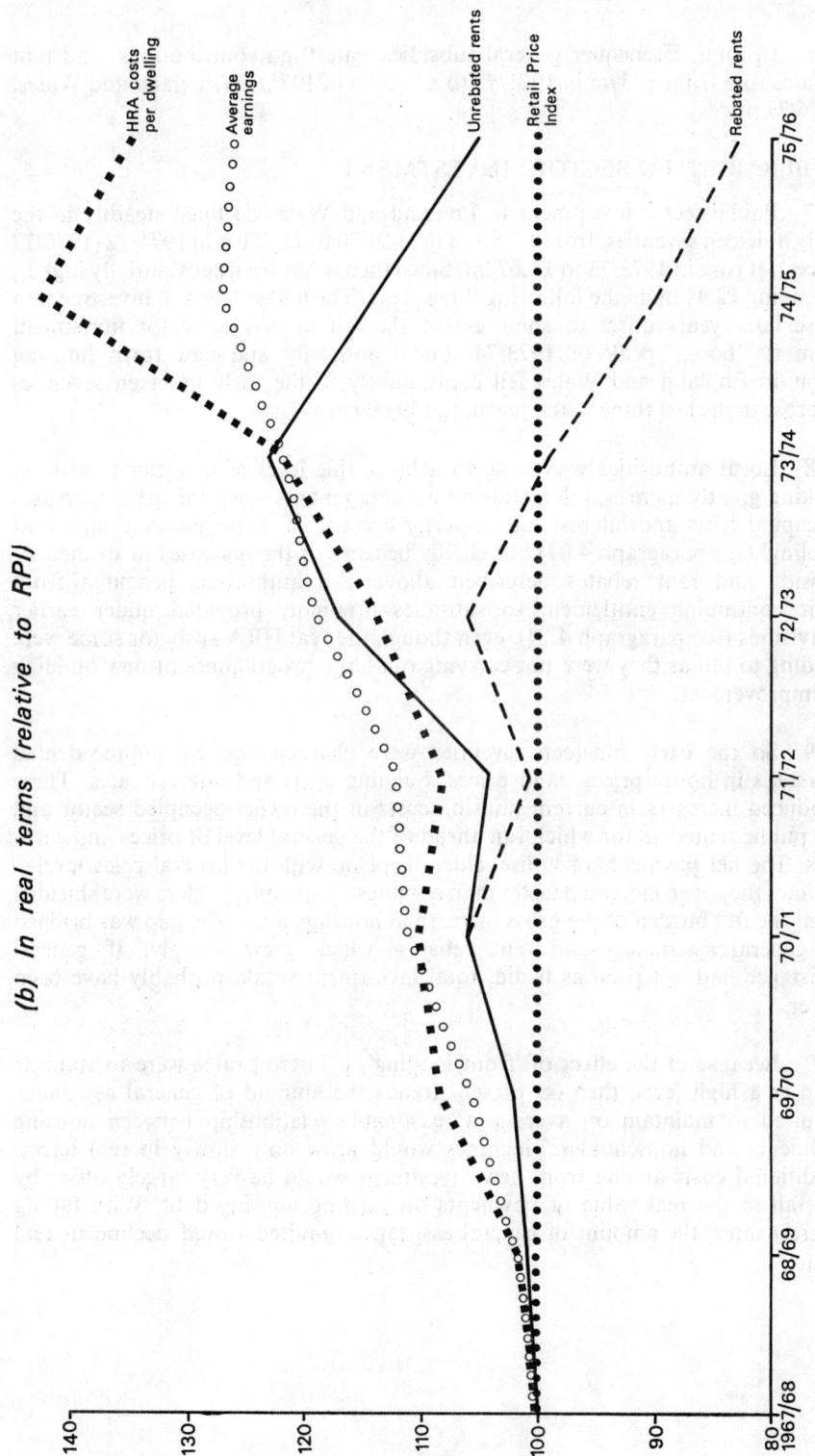

(b) In real terms (relative to RPI)

HRA costs per dwelling

Average earnings

Unrebated rents

Retail Price Index

Rebated rents

140
130
120
110
100
90
80

1967/68 68/69 69/70 70/71 71/72 72/73 73/74 74/75 75/76

Note

'Average earnings' are derived from the Department of Employment's monthly index of average pre-tax earnings of all employees, manual and non-manual.

4.26   In total, Exchequer general subsidies, rate fund contributions, and rent rebates rose from £459m in 1971/72 to £1,234m in 1975/76 (England and Wales, 1976/77 prices).

PUBLIC RENTED SECTOR: INVESTMENT

4.27   Public sector investment in England and Wales declined steadily in the early nineteen seventies, from £1,540m in 1969/70 to £1,370m in 1971/72 (1976/77 prices). It rose in 1972/73 to £1,672m. Since then it has been substantially higher, averaging £2,413m in the following three years. The higher levels of investment in these later years offset to some extent the fall in private sector investment from its 'boom' peak of 1973/74. Local authority and new town housing starts in England and Wales fell continuously in the early nineteen seventies but rose in the last three years, reaching 149,000 in 1976.

4.28   Local authorities were able to achieve this level of investment without making greatly increased demands on existing tenants—despite sharp increases in capital costs and interest rates—partly because of 'loans pooling' and 'rent pooling' (see paragraph 4.07) but chiefly because of the increases in Exchequer subsidy and rent rebates described above. All authorities benefited from their continuing entitlement to subsidies originally provided under earlier provisions (see paragraph 4.24), even though the real HRA costs for some were tending to fall as they were not carrying out large programmes of new building or improvement.

4.29   So the early nineteen seventies were characterised by unprecedented increases in house prices, land prices, building costs and interest rates. These produced increases in current housing costs in the owner-occupied sector and the public rented sector which ran ahead of the general level of prices and earnings. The net payments of householders kept up with the general price level— at times they even increased faster than earnings—but householders were shielded from the full burden of the gross increase in housing costs. The gap was bridged by general assistance—and rent rebates—which grew sharply. If general assistance had not risen as it did, total investment would probably have been lower.

4.30   Because of the effect of 'front loading', if interest rates were to stabilise even at a high level, then on present trends the amount of general assistance required to maintain on average a reasonable relationship between housing payments and householders' incomes would grow only slowly in real terms. Additional costs arising from new investment would be very largely offset by the fall in the real value of payments on existing housing debt. With falling interest rates, the amount of general assistance required would decline in real terms.

CHAPTER 5

Pricing and Assistance

5.01 As the previous chapter showed, increases in the cost of housing in the early nineteen seventies led to rapid changes in householders' outgoings. Some private and public sector tenants were protected against cost increases by income-related rent allowances and rent rebates. Most tenants of private landlords (or housing associations) had the benefit of rent control or rent regulation, which limited the scope for landlords to pass on cost increases. And the effect of cost increases was cushioned to some extent for public sector tenants and mortgagors by higher general assistance.

5.02 But the rise in general assistance not directly related to householders' incomes—in 1975/76 it averaged about £3 per week* for local authority tenants and for mortgagors—has prompted questions about how much people pay directly for their housing, how much help they get from the Exchequer, and how much they pay indirectly through taxation.

5.03 Under any financial arrangements for housing it is necessary to keep the level of assistance and its relation with housing costs, incomes, and householders' outgoings under review. The *level* of general assistance is however a separate question from the *basis* of general assistance. Recent debate has in part focussed on the case for changing the whole basis of providing assistance with housing payments, and for changing the pricing arrangements which determine householders' gross housing payments.

5.04 Four main proposals for change in the current basis of assistance and pricing which have figured in public discussion are that:

—general assistance should be *eliminated or substantially reduced and the rent rebate and rent allowance scheme extended;*

—general assistance should be replaced by a *universal flat rate personal housing allowance;*

—the gross housing payments of all householders—whether tenants or home owners—should be *related to the current value of their housing,* not to its historic cost;

—general housing assistance should be retained, but should be *distributed more fairly and more effectively.*

5.05 Radical changes in long-established financial arrangements are never easy. They are bound to cause problems for households who have planned their finances on the expectation that the current arrangements would continue. The question is whether the benefits of radical alternatives would sufficiently outweigh the advantages of the current forms of general assistance to justify the disruption that might be caused, no matter how carefully new arrangements were introduced.

---

*About £4 a week in 1976/77.

ASSISTANCE

General assistance

5.06 General assistance which meets some part of housing costs without regard to an individual householder's ability to pay is available in one form or another in many countries similar to our own, although there are wide variations in its scope and scale.

5.07 The annual cost of a typical new house has always been high in relation to average income—currently it is equal to about one-third of average earnings of male manual workers. By meeting a proportion of housing costs, general assistance enables a larger number of households to afford houses built or improved to acceptable contemporary standards without recourse to assistance based on individual tests of income and family circumstances. It makes possible higher housing standards than would otherwise be attained. It enables the provision of houses of good standard to be maintained in the face of increases in house prices and construction costs relative to incomes, and increases in interest rates.

5.08 Recent sharp increases in general assistance resulted from an unprecedented rise in the cost of housing. The harsh reality is that if the cost of housing rises sharply in relation to incomes, many people will be unwilling or unable to afford housing at present standards unless extra assistance is provided, in one way or another, to help them meet the extra cost.

5.09 But general assistance is by its very nature not directly related to ability to pay. Some householders therefore get more help than they strictly 'need' to enable them to afford a home of a decent basic standard. It is sometimes argued that general assistance:

—leads to over-investment in housing and wasteful use of the housing stock, and creates unreasonable expectations and artificial shortages;

—enables land owners and owners of existing houses to charge higher prices —although this is not readily quantifiable.

Elimination or Substantial Reduction of General Assistance

5.10 If general assistance from which public sector tenants and home owners with mortgages now benefit were substantially reduced, this would open the way to an equivalent reduction in the burden of taxation, Many more would benefit from tax reductions however than would pay for them through reduced general assistance. On average tenants in the public rented sector and home owners with mortgages would tend to pay more in extra charges for housing than they would get back in tax reductions, especially where there was only one earner in the household. Tenants in high cost areas or home owners with high percentage mortgages taken out recently would stand to lose most.

5.11 A large reduction in general assistance would affect both demand and supply in the housing market. The interactions could be complex, altering the level of effective demand, house prices and builders' profit margins. But the probable net outcome would be increased costs for the householder, leading to a reduction in effective demand and therefore lower investment in housing.

5.12 Less well-off householders might be safeguarded by adjustments to the rent rebate and rent allowance schemes, and perhaps by an extension of the scheme to home owners. But to the extent that lower income householders were protected against increased housing payments the net savings available for tax cuts would be reduced; and there would be much greater reliance on income-testing.

A Universal Housing Allowance

5.13 An alternative approach which would avoid an extension of personal income-tested assistance would be to abolish general assistance and replace it with a 'universal housing allowance'. This might for example take the form of a regular flat-rate payment made to all beneficiaries for as long as they remained householders. It would be large enough to enable the most hard-pressed families to afford housing of a reasonable basic standard. But it would be subject to income tax—so that a proportion would be 'clawed back' from the better-off by the workings of the tax system—and to this extent related to householders' incomes. It would replace both general and income-related housing assistance.

5.14 Such an arrangement raises serious practical problems:

—it would be difficult to define eligibility in numerous border-line cases— for example, would any single adult who wished to live independently qualify, and would those who owned their homes outright and no longer needed assistance qualify too?

—would recipients of the allowance be free to spend it on goods other than housing, accepting a lower standard of accommodation if they preferred to do so?

—the payment of a universal allowance, with income tax clawback, would involve a very large increase in the gross flow of payments in both directions, and a clawback through the tax system would not secure full repayment from those who did not need assistance;

—a fixed sum providing adequate help to householders with heavy housing costs would be more than adequate for others with lower costs; but if set at a lower level it would be insufficient for the many households with higher than average costs.

The first two of these objections might be overcome, although only by complex administrative mechanisms. But the last two are more difficult, especially the variation in the level of housing payments.

5.15 Housing costs vary widely, both over time and according to tenure and location. General assistance, which meets a proportion of borrowing costs, tends to reduce these variations. For example, a new mortgagor's initial mortgage payments consist almost entirely of interest which attracts tax relief. The interest element in his payments, and tax relief on interest, gradually fall until, when he has paid off his mortgage, he gets nothing. In the local authority sector, authorities with large current investment programmes and high costs are subsidised more heavily than those with lower costs (see paragraphs 4.05-4.10).

5.16 A flat rate allowance would not be able to cope with these differences in costs. If the allowance for all tenants and home owners had been introduced in 1975/76 at a level of, say, £280 a year—the basic rate tax relief on an average mortgage taken by first-time purchasers—the total cost would have been some £5,700m gross (before any tax claw back) (United Kingdom figures). This is over twice the total amount of general assistance actually paid. Even so, half a million mortgagors and at least as many public rented sector tenants would have been worse off—even if none of the allowance had been clawed back through tax—unless income-tested subsidies had been provided as well.

5.17 Because of the problem of the wide variation in householders' payments under present arrangements, the introduction of a consistent basis of pricing in all housing sectors—based on current values—might be regarded as a necessary prior step to the introduction of a universal housing allowance unrelated to income or actual housing payments.

PRICING

5.18 As noted in Chapter 4, the borrowing costs on a house depend primarily on the 'historic' cost—the price originally paid by the current owner. Over time, the historic cost diverges from the current value—sharply in periods of high inflation—so that the borrowing costs on a house purchased some years ago are a good deal lower than those of newly-purchased houses of similar quality.

5.19 For most goods and services the price paid reflects the current value; and for investment goods any difference between historic costs and current values is reflected in taxable profits and so is subject to tax. But for both public sector tenants and home owners the divergence between outgoings derived from historic costs and the outgoings that would fully reflect current values is not subject to tax. The effects are different in the two main sectors. In the public sector, the benefits are 'pooled' (see paragraph 4.07) leading to a lower average level of rents. Home owners benefit individually, and their payments start higher and tend to fall in real terms. The overall effect for both public sector tenants and home owners is that on average their regular payments for housing are lower in relation to the supply cost of new houses than would be the case with most other goods.

5.20 Most tenants of private landlords and housing associations pay 'fair rents'. These may be closer to current values, but local 'scarcity factors' are excluded and the system of rent revisions means that 'fair rents' tend to lag behind 'market' rents, especially when increases are phased over several years.

5.21 Current value pricing in the public rented sector would probably involve assessing 'market' rents by analogy with privately-rented dwellings. Such assessments are not impossible but tend to be arbitrary since in many areas there are too few houses let at market-related rents to provide a benchmark. In the

34

owner-occupied sector, current value pricing would probably involve the taxation of notional income from 'beneficial occupation'—an amount related to the difference between outgoings actually incurred and the current market rental.

5.22 The case against 'historic' pricing is that it distorts the financial basis of choice. Because payments for housing are on average lower in relation to its current value than is the case with most other goods, people expect and get more, and a large share of resources goes to housing. The different patterns of payments in the two main sectors are difficult to compare. Mobility may be restricted in cases where the benefits of the divergence of historic cost and current values are reduced or lost if a householder moves.

5.23 For those able to pay current values without assistance, or with the assistance of a universal housing allowance, current value pricing could provide a less distorted basis for choice. But for many low income households, especially those in high cost areas, a universal housing allowance at any feasible level would be insufficient, unless supported by additional income-tested assistance. The advantages of current value pricing in improving the basis for choice have to be balanced against:

—*The effects on housing investment.* Gross payments by householders based on current values would be substantially higher than their present gross payments based on historic costs. Such a pricing regime would tend to reduce the demand for housing and lead to the diversion of some expenditure currently devoted to housing into other channels. The universal housing allowance might be pitched high enough to offset much of the price increase for the majority of householders. But this would be costly (see paragraph 5.16); and the more subsidy was used to compensate for higher prices, the less would current value pricing achieve the objective of an allocation of resources to housing based on willingness and ability to pay.

—*Upheaval in the household budgets of millions of families.* Even if the total volume of assistance to householders remained the same, the distribution would be very different—for example, in the owner-occupied sector, older home owners who had paid up their mortgages would be hardest hit by the introduction of a tax on their notional income from beneficial occupation.

—*Uncertainty.* If there were continuing doubt about the permanence of so radical a change, this could cause pervasive and disruptive uncertainty for householders, local authorities and housebuilders.

—*The doubtful social justification.* Current value pricing would involve taxing housing in the owner-occupied sector, and treating it as a profit making asset in the public sector.

—*The very heavy administrative costs and complications.* They would be unavoidable.

5.24 The Government conclude that it would be better to retain the present structure of pricing and general assistance rather than replace it with radically different arrangements. No system of housing finance is flawless. General assistance has its imperfections. But its disadvantages can be lessened if a sensible relationship is maintained between current housing costs and householders' incomes, and levels of assistance.

MORE EFFECTIVE USE OF GENERAL ASSISTANCE

Public rented sector subsidy and rents

5.25   There is a wide disparity in the level of housing costs falling on local authority Housing Revenue Accounts, and consequently in the level of rents paid by their tenants, as the following table for English authorities shows:

TABLE 2

SIZE OF GOVERNMENT AND LOCAL CONTRIBUTIONS TO HOUSING REVENUE ACCOUNT EXPENDITURE: RANGE BETWEEN AUTHORITIES WITH HIGHEST AND LOWEST EXPENDITURE, 1975/76 (OUTTURN PRICES)

	Average expenditure £ per dwelling	Authority with the highest average expenditure £ per dwelling		Authority with the lowest average expenditure £ per dwelling	
	England	Greater London	Rest of England	Greater London	Rest of England
Total expenditure/income ...	419	1,120	861	383	227
Government subsidies ...	132	547	493	71	40
Gross rents	225	284	252	277	173
Rate Fund contributions ...	36	260	100	2	1

Note: Items do not add up to totals because of other minor sources of income not shown and changes in working balances.

This is primarily because of differences in the age structure of a local authority's housing stock and capital debt, which is strongly affected by its current programme of investment in housing. Disparities in rent levels are accentuated by the fact that all local authorities, irrespective of their present circumstances, receive annual subsidies on a basis which does not take full account of recent changes in prices, incomes and interest rates.

5.26   The Government believe that there is a need for a new public sector subsidy system designed to achieve a more efficient and fairer use of subsidy. This could be done by reducing subsidy in areas where the need for it is declining in order to concentrate it more on authorities who need large investment programmes and whose costs are consequently rising.

5.27   The Government consider that the right to fix rents must be left in the hands of locally elected representatives and that rents should continue to be set on a non profit making basis. Local authorities should retain their freedom to supplement Exchequer subsidy with a contribution from the General Rate Fund.

5.28   Although in the long run rents and housing costs must stand in reasonable relationship, the Government do not consider that it is sensible to think in terms of rents meeting some fixed proportion of housing costs in each and every year. Housing costs falling on local authority accounts can fluctuate widely from year to year in real terms. It would be unreasonable to expect rents to move immediately to the full extent of such fluctuations.

36

5.29 The Government therefore propose for the purposes of determining subsidy to settle annually, in consultation with the local authority representatives, the contribution to housing costs which can reasonably be expected from local resources. All relevant factors, such as past and expected movements in incomes, costs and prices, would be brought into the reckoning. This should avoid the need for irregular and sharp changes in rent levels. The Government consider that over a run of years rents should keep broadly in line with changes in money incomes. The proposed new subsidy system is fully discussed in Chapter 9.

Home ownership—mortgage payments and tax relief on interest

5.30 The Government consider that tax relief on mortgage interest—which has a long history as part of the tax structure—and the option mortgage subsidy must form an integral part of their housing policy. The continuance of mortgage tax relief and option mortgage subsidy is vital to the growth of home ownership.

5.31 The assumed benefit of owning a house used to be treated as notional income for tax purposes under Schedule A of the Income Tax Acts. This was abolished in 1963. In 1974 the Government ended tax relief on interest on most forms of personal loans other than for house purchase and improvement; limited to £25,000 the amount of a housing loan on which tax relief is available; and ended tax relief on mortgage interest in respect of second homes subject to transitional arrangements.

5.32 The value of tax relief to the individual varies not only with the size of a mortgage, but also with the form of a mortgage, the rate of interest payable, current tax rates and the mortgagor's marginal tax rate. At the basic rate of tax, about one-third of annual interest charges are offset by tax relief. Option mortgage subsidy provides roughly the same proportion of assistance as tax relief at the basic rate. This is especially important for the house-buyer whose income is not high enough to qualify for tax relief on the whole of his mortgage interest.

5.33 In 1976/77 there were about 6 million homes owned on mortgage and about £10¼ million home owners in the United Kingdom. The cost of tax relief on mortgage interest was £980m in 1975/76* (United Kingdom, 1976/77 prices); the cost of option mortgage subsidy was £120m in 1975/76 (Great Britain, 1976/77 prices).

5.34 Average tax relief on mortgage interest (including option mortgage subsidy) per mortgaged house was £186 in 1975/76 (1976/77 prices)†. Average figures of course conceal wide variations. There are geographical differences in house prices and therefore in the size of mortgages. Even more important are variations in mortgages related to the date at which the house was purchased. Because of inflation the more recent the date of purchase the higher the price will have tended to be, and often the bigger mortgages will be associated with these recent purchases, especially by first-time buyers. So the pattern of mortgage interest relief tends to be that people who bought a first house in recent years,

*Mortgage tax relief and option mortgage subsidy were £1,100m and £140m respectively in 1976/77.

†Average assistance per mortgaged house was £205 in 1976/77.

or moved to another house for one reason or another, are getting most benefit from the tax relief—though they will be paying a higher net amount—while those who have lived a long period in their house and paid off their mortgage no longer get any benefit at all. This pattern is the more marked because it is a characteristic of the commonest form of mortgage that tax relief is proportionately largest in the initial years of a loan.

5.35 It has been argued that mortgage tax relief—whatever may be said about it in relation to the principles of taxation—has become a form of special assistance to house purchase because of the changes referred to in paragraph 5.31. Proposals have therefore been advanced from time to time for limiting the amount of tax relief on mortgage interest which can be obtained; not only on 'second homes', for which mortgage tax relief is no longer available apart from the transitional arrangements, but also on the 'principal' home.

5.36 Thus it has been argued that whilst tax relief on mortgage interest is necessary for first-time buyers, because initial costs are high in relation to average incomes, such relief is less necessary for people buying subsequent homes. A 'single annuity' mortgage has been proposed such that on moving to a subsequent house a person's relief would be calculated as if his new mortgage had been running ever since his first purchase. Another possibility advanced for limiting the amount of assistance given to the individual is the restriction of mortgage tax relief to the basic rate of tax, whether the mortgagor is a first-time house-buyer or not.

5.37 The Government have carefully considered the proposals of these kinds. But they are open to serious objections:

(i) The 'single annuity' proposal recognises the importance of mortgage tax relief to first-time house-buyers. But it can be just as important to existing mortgagors who move house—for example, to take up a new job, to be nearer relations, or to buy a largei house to accommodate a growing family. So a general restriction of mortgage tax relief as envisaged in the 'single annuity' proposal could be very harmful both in social and economic terms—its effect on job mobility could be especially damaging. Moreover the administration would be very difficult—records of everybody's mortgage history would be required.

(ii) As for the tax relief at the higher rates on mortgage interest, this benefit is no longer confined to a tiny minority—even some first-time house-buyers benefit—because of the effects of inflation in relation to tax thresholds. About $\frac{3}{4}$ million mortgagors qualified for tax relief at the higher rates totalling about £90m in 1975/76 (1976/77 prices).* About $\frac{3}{4}$ million mortgagors will still qualify for such relief in 1977/78 despite the raising of tax thresholds in the last budget. Moreover most of those who benefit from mortgage tax relief at the higher rates earn 'middle' rather than 'high' incomes—the higher tax rates begin to take effect at a gross annual income in the range of £7,000–£8,000.

(iii) Any significant reduction in mortgage tax relief—whether through a 'single annuity' or similar arrangements, or withdrawal of tax relief at the higher rates—would be damaging to individuals, even with transitional arrangements. People who buy their homes on mortgage do so

*1 million mortgagors qualified for £120 million tax relief at the higher rates in 1976/77.

after careful consideration of their likely household income and expenditure over many years ahead. The withdrawal of tax relief entitlements which have evolved *not* as part of housing policy but as part of a progressive taxation structure would be unfair and could result in hardship to a large number of families. The social justice of a system of taxation should be judged by the totality of the system, not by any one element within it. Any allowance or relief that can be set against total income before tax can be criticised as 'regressive' when the tax is levied on a graduated scale. But the total impact of the British system of income tax is highly progressive.

(iv) Reduced tax relief on mortgage interest would also disrupt the housing market as its effects would not be confined only to those who would directly lose. In the upper part of the housing market demand would fall and supply rise, while in the lower part the reverse would happen; and the changes would be reflected in prices. The market would adjust over time. How long this would take is uncertain, but in the meantime some buyers would be squeezed out; there would be a lower level of housebuilding; and some builders would suffer losses, as would some home owners.

5.38 The Government do not therefore consider that there is a case on grounds of housing policy for an alteration to present arrangements governing tax relief on mortgage interest and option mortgage subsidy. The Government intend to maintain a limit, at present £25,000, on that part of loans for house purchase admissible for tax relief; this limit, which has to be fixed annually, will be kept under review. As regards Schedule A type or imputed income taxation, the Government would see the gravest administrative difficulties about reintroducing it. Apart from these difficulties, however, and the question of public acceptability, such a tax would again be incompatible in their view with their strategy for the growth of home ownership (see paragraphs 5.18–5.24).

COMPARISONS OF ASSISTANCE TO HOME OWNERS AND LOCAL AUTHORITY TENANTS

5.39 A rigorous approach to comparisons of home owners and local authority tenants would involve drawing up a 'balance sheet' of actual and imputed costs and benefits of householders in the two sectors to establish a neutral position from which the provision of assistance can be judged. But there is *no* neutral position. Any comparison involves judgements about whether or not to include in the balance sheet large and contentious items—for example, the absence of a tax on 'notional income' from home ownership, and the use of historic costs rather than market values in setting council rents. There is no objective basis for deciding these questions.*

5.40 Most of the recent debate on equity between the main sectors has centred on a more limited question—whether the Government are providing broadly the same help to both sectors in the form of mortgage tax relief and public sector general housing subsidies.

5.41 But what is 'the same'? A higher level of assistance to local authorities in high cost areas faced with pressing housing needs can be justified on grounds

*See Technical Volume, Chapter 5.

of social policy. Nevertheless, comparisons are commonly made in terms of the total amount of assistance to each sector or the amount of assistance 'per head'. The estimated figures for 1975/76 are:

TABLE 3

GENERAL ASSISTANCE, 1975/76 (1976/77 PRICES)

	Numbers (m)	Amount (£m)	Amount per head (£)*
Local authority tenants (England and Wales)† ...	4·7	915	195
All home owners (UK)	10·0	1,100	110
All mortgaged houses (UK)	5·9	1,100	185

*Estimated figures for 1976/77 are: local authority tenants 4·8m; total assistance £1,015m; amount per head £210; all home owners 10·2m; total assistance £1,240m; amount per head £120; all mortgaged houses 6m; amount per head £205.

†1·9 million local authority tenants received an estimated £250m in rent rebates in 1975/76, an average of £130 per recipient (1976/77 prices); estimated figures for 1976/77 are 2 million tenants receiving £275m or £140 per recipient.

5.42   Average figures are however of limited value. There are detailed problems of comparison—for example, should all home owners or only mortgagors be included? But there is a more fundamental weakness to this approach. The amount of general assistance depends on the level of costs in each sector. The numerical equivalence at any point in time of assistance in the two sectors, either in terms of the total or amount per head, would be fortuitous. The sectors are very different in size, and different rates of growth of the sectors and other extraneous factors affect the balance. For example, as home ownership is growing faster, proportionately more new debt is being taken on at current house values. So total assistance and average assistance per head are rising faster than in the public sector.

5.43   An alternative approach might be to focus on the rate of assistance provided towards interest payments. This is the one form of assistance from which both home owners and public sector tenants benefit; and it might provide the basis for forging a reasonable link between them. Thus, home owners continue to be eligible for tax relief irrespective of any individual need for assistance so long as they have a mortgage outstanding and interest payments to make. Similarly, under the new public sector subsidy system, it might be considered desirable to have some minimum provision to ensure that all individual authorities continue to receive some general assistance in the years ahead. So one possibility would be to introduce some link between the rate of tax relief and the local authority minimum entitlement to subsidy.

5.44   Comparisons of assistance stretching ahead into the future have sometimes been held to show that it is a 'better buy' in terms of public finance to provide a new house in the owner-occupied sector rather than in the public sector. Under present arrangements general subsidy on a new local authority house is greater in the early years than mortgage tax relief on a similar house bought

40

for home ownership. But thereafter the value of tax relief tends to remain reasonably steady in real terms as the owner-occupied house is 'revalued' through sale and repurchase at current prices, while the value of subsidy on the local authority house tends to fall in real terms. The true cost to the taxpayer lies in the amount of general assistance paid in respect of those houses over the whole of their useful life—conventionally assumed to be 60 years. To calculate this in 'net present value' terms, assumptions must be made about interest rates, rent levels, house prices, and taxation policy over the whole period. The 'leverage' of initial assumptions about interest rates and other financial factors compounded over a 60 year period is very big. A relatively small change in the initial assumptions—for example about rates of increase in rents —greatly alters the results.

5.45 A further objection to this kind of comparison is that although it recognises the contribution of home ownership towards meeting housing requirements, it ignores the special role of the public sector in dealing with the most pressing problems. If a public sector authority provides a new house it will normally allocate it to someone at the head of its waiting list—for example a family rehoused from an unfit house or a household living in overcrowded conditions. There could be no guarantee that if the same new house were built for owner-occupation it would be sold to someone in equally pressing housing need. Consequently, even if home ownership were a 'better buy' in terms of cost to the taxpayer, there would be heavy social costs incurred in concentrating almost exclusively on building for home ownership.

CONCLUSIONS ON PRICING AND ASSISTANCE

5.46 The present financial system, with pricing based on historic costs in the owner-occupied and public rented sectors coupled with general assistance, does have disadvantages. These arrangements may lead to some rigidity in the housing market and may not secure maximum efficiency in the use of resources, or fairness between individuals. But radical alternatives pose formidable problems both of principle and practice. Moreover, current arrangements have been woven into the long-term plans of most householders. It would not be reasonable to replace them unless the case for doing so was overwhelming.

5.47 Although the drawbacks of general assistance cannot be eliminated they can be moderated if a reasonable relationship is maintained between current housing costs and householders' incomes, and levels of general assistance. Moreover, the burden of general assistance will grow lighter if interest rates in the years ahead are steadier than in recent years. A more effective and fairer use of general assistance could be achieved by a new public sector subsidy system more closely related to needs, by maintaining and keeping under review the ceiling of £25,000 on the amount of mortgage eligible for tax relief, and possibly by some link between the rate of assistance towards interest payments in the two main sectors.

Part III: The Future

CHAPTER 6

A National Housing Policy

6.01   A housing policy designed to achieve the Government's housing objectives—set out in Chapter 2 (paragraphs 2.16–2.19)—must be flexible enough to withstand the strain of unforeseen developments and to accommodate a wide range of other social and economic policies. The individual parts of a national housing policy must also be closely interrelated. Achievement of all the objectives ultimately depends on a reasonably adequate supply of housing. And a single policy initiative will often serve several ends—for example, wider access to home ownership will help to meet the preferences of many people, will ease the pressures in the public sector, and will allow for more flexible use of the housing stock.

6.02   This chapter outlines the main elements in the Government's housing policy.

LOCAL HOUSING STRATEGIES

6.03   Local authorities have a statutory duty to review the housing conditions of their areas. This duty used to be interpreted primarily as identifying what needed to be done in the public sector. This was right when virtually every authority was confronted with an absolute shortage of housing. But times have changed. Housing conditions now vary widely up and down the country.

6.04   In this situation it is unrealistic for Westminster and Whitehall to attempt to lay down in detail what action should be taken locally, or for local authorities to interpret their role too narrowly. We need a new relationship between central and local levels of Government, which more accurately reflects changing circumstances. Central Government must lay down an overall national policy framework, and provide advice where necessary. But the key to the success of national housing policy now lies in the development of effective *local* housing strategies, planned and carried out by local authorities with the minimum of detailed intervention from the centre.

6.05   Local authorities need to make assessments of the full range of housing requirements in their areas. Only they can take this broad view. Many authorities are already trying to do this, and are building up the necessary body of information. Others will have to draw on statistics which are sometimes out of date and incomplete. But they will be able to provide from experience the essential information about the character of local problems which cannot be deduced from national statistics. Against this background, each local authority should draw up a strategic statement backed by statistics on the local housing stock and households and expected changes over the next few years, and a programme for its own proposed housing investment (see paragraphs 6.12–6.16 below).

6.06   In working out the local housing strategy, local authorities will need to take account of policies in other fields—such as transport and employment, health and social services—within the broad framework of the development plans for the area. It is particularly important for local authorities to develop their housing strategies in close co-ordination with social service and health authorities, so that adequate housing arrangements can be made for those with particular problems such as the elderly, the disabled and the handicapped who need special help.

6.07   Local authorities will want to make sure that there is land available to match their own housing development needs and those of other public agencies. They will also need to ensure that demands for land for private housebuilding are met, either by making land available themselves, or by land ready and available on the open market. Local authorities have a duty under the Community Land Act to have regard to the needs of builders and developers. It is possible, given the housing objective of achieving an optimum balance between investment on new houses and the improvement and better use of older ones, that in some places the need for land for new housebuilding may decline as the emphasis shifts from redevelopment to rehabilitation. In some areas, the need for any increase in the supply of housing may gradually ease off or may already have done so. In other areas, new developments may take a more prominent place, whether on green field sites or as piecemeal or small-scale redevelopment. But factors such as these are essentially local, and will need to be taken regularly into account in investment programmes and land policy statements, along with the changing patterns of transport and land use for the area as a whole.

6.08   The local authority's own investment programme will often lie at the heart of the local housing strategy. But the local housing strategy must go much wider. In many areas public rented sector provision will provide only some of the answers. The right local mix of solutions will involve action by all concerned with rented and owner-occupied housing. It will require not only investment in new and improved housing, but also initiatives to help people obtain the sort of housing they want—this may involve some re-ordering of priorities both by public sector bodies and by mortgage lenders. The local authorities will need to develop their existing working relationships with all other bodies—the Housing Corporation, registered housing associations, local housebuilders, building societies, new town corporations, county councils and tenants' and community organisations—concerned with housing in their areas.

6.09   Policy changes arising from this Green Paper must make a full contribution to the problems of inner city areas, particularly where the familiar problems of decay and neglect are compounded by high building costs and a persistent lack of housing of acceptable standards. The recent White Paper on inner city policy (Cmnd 6845) made clear that the Government intend to give priority to local authorities with severe inner area housing problems. In preparing programmes and policies for inner city areas authorities will be expected to co-ordinate their housing strategy with other proposals for regeneration.

6.10   The new towns still have an important contribution to make. There remains a need for them to help with the problems of the inner cities. The

Government's aim is to strike the right balance between development in the cities themselves and development outside them, particularly in the new towns; and to ensure that the new towns provide for as wide a cross-section of people as possible—for the elderly and the disadvantaged as well as the skilled and the productive—by making houses available both for renting and buying.

6.11 The Government propose to establish a Housing Consultative Council (HCC) for England, with representatives of the local authorities and the Department of the Environment under the chairmanship of the Secretary of State for the Environment, to consider all major issues of concern to local authorities in the performance of their housing duties. Existing Government consultative machinery involving other bodies concerned with housing, such as the building societies and housebuilders, will be maintained and developed. Joint discussions between the HCC and other bodies will be arranged when necessary. In Wales, the existing relationship with the Council of the Principality will be continued and developed.

HOUSING INVESTMENT

6.12 We still need a substantial level of housing investment in both the Public and the private sectors to help deal with poor housing conditions and special housing needs, and to provide for future growth in the number of households.

6.13 The level of private investment in housing—notably for home ownership—is largely determined by the level of effective demand. The Government can influence it, but do not control it. The level of investment in housing in the public sector however its primarily a matter for Government decision. The public sector will continue to play the major part in dealing with the most pressing housing problems. Public resources must be used economically and efficiently, and applied where most needed.

6.14 The Government therefore propose to institute and develop a system of local authority housing investment programmes (HIPs). These will be drawn up as part of the local housing strategy. They will set out the authority's proposals for investment in the whole range of its housing activities for the following four years, within the context of the expected activity of other public housing bodies in the area and private housebuilders. The HIPs will be revised each year. This system will make it possible to identify the most urgent problems, and to allocate resources to each authority on the basis of informed judgements of priorities. A corresponding system will be further developed in Wales.

6.15 These arrangements should enable a faster rate of progress to be made—for any given level of housing investment—in dealing with the most acute housing problems. Naturally, the overall rate of progress will be influenced by the speed of economic recovery.

6.16 In the course of the next decade a growing number of local authorities should have very largely dealt with their backlog of bad housing conditions. As this occurs, the overall level of public sector housing investment should decline in response to changing circumstances. The danger of coming to premature and false conclusions, based on inadequate information, about the appropriate level of investment will be avoided by the regular monitoring of progress under local housing strategies and housing investment programmes.

FINANCIAL STABILITY

6.17 Rapid inflation and large rises in interest rates—and changes in the relationship between them—can play havoc with any housing policy unless we have a financial structure that will withstand such strains.

6.18 The Government are giving high priority to the control of inflation; success in that effort will go far to reduce the risk of a recurrence of the events of 1971–74. But arrangements for housing finance must be robust enough to cope with major shifts in prices and interest rates. In the public sector the Government propose a more flexible system of subsidy (see paragraphs 5.25–5.29 and 6.39).

6.19 In the owner-occupied sector we need to maintain mortgage tax relief and option mortgage subsidy and to secure as far as possible a supply of mortgage funds which is not subject to sharp short-term fluctuations, and increases sufficiently over the years to meet fresh demands (see paragraphs 5.30–5.38 and 6.40).

6.20 To prevent short term disruptions of the private housing market that are harmful both to householders and to the housebuilding industry the Government will develop the present arrangements with the building societies for stabilising the supply of mortgage funds. To guard against the risk that in the years ahead societies may not be able to secure all the finance that they need directly from the personal sector, the Government wish to discuss with the societies the possibility of their securing fresh sources of funds, possibly through a financial intermediary. The Government will also seek the views of the Committee to Review Financial Institutions (the Wilson Committee) on this proposal in due course.

THE HOUSEHOLDER—TENURE

6.21 *Home ownership.* People from all walks of life aspire to own their own homes, but in the past home ownership was confined to the better-off. With rising standards of living this is changing, and many of those now entering this sector are families who in former times might have considered home ownership to be beyond their reach. Home ownership now crosses social boundaries; for example more skilled manual workers are home owners than local authority tenants.

6.22 The Government welcome this trend towards home ownership, which gives many people the kind of home they want. It reduces the demands made on the public sector. It helps with problems of mobility, particularly for people who need to move to a new area when changing jobs.

6.23 The Government will therefore promote measures to widen still further the opportunities for home ownership, including a special scheme of Government assistance for first-time buyers.

6.24 The Government also look to building societies and other lenders to provide forms of mortgage facility which are more helpful to people with modest incomes, and to lend more to lower income applicants and on cheaper properties—particularly in inner city areas. Increased 'down market' lending by building societies will involve a close working relationship between the societies and local authorities.

6.25 Many local authority tenants wish to become home owners, and there can be advantages in an authority allowing a tenant to buy the house he rents if he so wishes. If he is prevented from doing so he may move out of the area altogether, while in buying his present home he may help develop a variety of tenure within the neighbourhood, which the Government would encourage. The Government are therefore not opposed to sales of council houses provided that they can be made without impairing an authority's ability to deal with pressing housing needs or to maintain a housing stock of adequate quality for renting. But they cannot accept indiscriminate and unregulated programmes of sales in areas where pressure for houses to rent remains high and where the authority is not taking compensating action to keep up the supply of adequate housing for rent. This would damage the prospects of a decent home for those in need. The judgment on whether to sell should therefore be set within a balanced assessment of local housing need and the strategy to meet it.

6.26 *New forms of tenure*. The Government also wish to encourage newer forms of tenure, such as equity sharing (part rent, part mortgage), co-ownership, and housing co-operatives. Housing associations and local authorities will have an important part to play in promoting schemes of this kind. There may also be some scope for developing alternative forms of tenure in the private sector.

6.27 *Renting*. For many, renting will continue to be the best arrangement. This includes those who prefer to rent, and those who cannot buy, even under the proposed measures to widen access to home ownership. It also includes those who need to obtain accommodation on a relatively temporary basis at some stage, not as a permanent home.

6.28 There is scope for sustaining and perhaps in some areas augmenting the supply of certain types of private letting—for example by encouraging home owners to let spare rooms, or temporarily absent home owners to let their house, by making it easier for them to recover possession; and by encouraging local authorities to ease restrictions on sub-letting by their tenants. The Review of the Rent Acts may suggest other approaches. But it seems clear that the importance of the social landlords—local authorities, registered housing associations, and new towns—will continue to grow.

6.29 Local authorities have become and will remain the chief providers of rented accommodation. Before 1939 they were required to provide for the housing needs of 'the working classes'. That limitation was removed from the statute in 1949. The Government do not intend to move back to the days when housing tenure was a matter of social class. Local authorities cater for a wide cross-section of the population. The Government believe that they must continue to do so, and must also continue to shoulder a particular responsibility for those with specialised or urgent needs.

6.30 Local authorities have for some years now been extending their traditional role of providing housing for families with children in the face of the changing pattern of household types—in particular the increase in elderly one-person households—and the decline of the private rented sector. They are increasingly providing special housing for groups such as frail elderly people and the disabled and for individuals in very pressing need such as certain one parent families. But in addition they will want to consider the claims of people who have not previously been given high priority in waiting lists. These will include for example young and middle aged single people, and mobile workers, apprentices and students, who need accommodation for a limited period. This will involve a liberalisation of local authority tenancy allocation and transfer policies, to ensure that the claims of these people as well as those of longstanding residents are considered on their merits. As pressures ease in particular areas, local authorities will be able to do more to help such people. The newly emerging needs must be taken into account in local authorities' overall housing strategies.

6.31 The responsibilities of most local authorities and the problems they face will continue to be formidable, and there will be difficult judgements about priorities.

6.32 The Government intend to continue their support for registered housing associations. Housing associations, in co-operation with local authorities, can offer an important element of choice in socially owned rented housing, and are able to specialise in dealing with groups such as mobile key workers, the elderly and the disabled.

THE HOUSEHOLDER—FREEDOM FROM RESTRICTIONS

6.33 The financial liabilities of home owners and tenants are different; consequently their rights and responsibilities are different. But it is wrong to regard tenancy as in any sense inferior to ownership. The Government propose to develop a 'Tenants' Charter' to safeguard and extend tenants' rights in both public and private sectors.

6.34 In the public sector, tenants should have security of tenure and better tenancy agreements than are often provided now. They should be freed from unnecessarily restrictive management practices.

6.35 There is an urgent need for a general improvement in the quality of local authority housing management and maintenance. Where in the past the answer to many housing problems was simply to build more houses, in the future it will increasingly lie in more careful consideration of the needs and problems of tenants and better use and upkeep of the existing housing stock. All authorities should aim to reach the standards of the best. The Department of the Environment has already established a Housing Services Advisory Group to give advice on housing management practice. In particular, local authorities should seek means of achieving greater tenant involvement in housing management—including the development of management co-operatives. Certain estates have a high incidence of social, economic and physical problems, and a higher level of expenditure may be needed on both management and maintenance. Local authorities with these 'problem' estates must be enabled to maintain expenditure at higher levels, without unduly stretching their resources.

6.36 The Review of the Rent Acts provides the opportunity for similar improvements in the rights of private tenants. Private tenants already have legal security of tenure. But the Government intend to explore ways of improving their position—for example by giving them the right to obtain grants towards the improvement of their homes, and to purchase their own homes, where blocks of flats are offered for sale and this can be done within a co-operative framework.

RENEWAL

6.37 In the nineteen fifties and nineteen sixties, large-scale demolition and the building of big new council estates was often thought to be the only quick way of dealing with problems of slums and shortages. Great improvements in housing conditions were achieved, though not always in the environment. But the effects on established communities were sometimes disastrous. We do not need and cannot afford to repeat these mistakes. The Government believe that housing policy should foster and reinforce the development of existing community ties. It will be important to bear this in mind in planning the regeneration of inner city areas.

6.38 There can be no clear-cut rule that renovation is better than new building. The best course will often be a careful mixture of the two. It is too soon to assess the results of the 1974 Housing Act, which was meant to encourage this approach. But meanwhile, local authorities will be given advice on choosing between renovation and demolition—taking account of social costs—and asked to concentrate their renovation budgets so far as possible on basic improvements to fundamentally sound houses which might otherwise be lost through neglect, rather than on high quality renovation of relatively small numbers of houses.

ASSISTANCE WITH HOUSING COSTS

(i) Public Sector Subsidy

6.39 The Government propose to hold consultations with the local authority representatives and other bodies about replacement of the present interim arrangements by a new public sector subsidy system, which is fully described in Chapter 9. We need to secure a more effective and fairer use of subsidy. This can be done through a system which concentrates subsidy on authorities with pressing housing needs—who will consequently have large investment programmes—and avoids the need for irregular and sharp changes in rent levels. As indicated in paragraph 5.29, the Government consider that over a run of years rents should keep broadly in line with changes in money incomes.

(ii) Mortgage Tax Relief

6.40 The Government are firmly committed to the continuance of tax relief on mortgage interest and option mortgage subsidy. This is essential if the steady growth of home ownership is to be maintained. The £25,000 ceiling on loans for house purchase limits the amount of tax relief which an individual mortgagor can get; and this limit will be kept under review.

(iii) Fairness between tenures

6.41 Much of the debate on 'equity' in housing is sterile: it is an attempt to compare chalk and cheese. The question of comparing the full range of benefits of home ownership and renting was briefly discussed in Chapter 5. There are fundamental differences between the two tenures which must defeat any attempt to draw up an incontrovertible 'balance sheet'.

6.42 It does seem right, however, to look for some approach to the provision of general assistance to both main tenures that would be generally accepted as broadly fair. A possible answer might be to provide powers to prescribe a *minimum* rate of general subsidy towards local authority interest payments related to the basic rate of tax relief on mortgage interest. The Government would welcome public discussion of this possibility.

(iv) Income Related Assistance

6.43 The Government have decided to retain the existing rent rebates and rent allowances, though a further study of these and other forms of income-related housing assistance is taking place. Only minor changes seem necessary in the meantime, such as standardisation of the rate of central Government's contribution to the two forms of assistance.

6.44 Specific policy proposals are more fully discussed in subsequent chapters.

CHAPTER 7

Home Ownership

7.01 An increasing number of people want to own their own home. The Government welcome this trend and—as indicated in Chapter 5—intend to continue to support home ownership by maintaining the current arrangements for tax relief and option mortgage subsidy.

7.02 Before the First World War, home ownership was the prerogative of the few, but during the late nineteen fifties it became the largest form of tenure. By 1971, 52 per cent of all houses in England and Wales were owner-occupied; the estimated figure for 1976 is 55 per cent—10 million out of 18·1 million.

7.03 A preference for home ownership is sometimes explained on the grounds that potential home owners believe that it will bring them financial advantage. A far more likely reason for the secular trend towards home ownership is the sense of greater personal independence that it brings. For most people owning one's own home is a basic and natural desire, which for more and more people is becoming attainable.

7.04 House purchase is generally achieved by means of loans from one of three main lending institutions—the building societies, local authorities and insurance companies—who together finance about 90 per cent of house purchases by first-time buyers, and 70-75 per cent of other house purchases. But the main source of funds is the building societies. In recent years they have provided between 80 per cent and 95 per cent of all advances for house purchases by the three main lending institutions, in terms both of the value and the number of advances.*

7.05 The building societies have come a long way since their beginnings in the nineteenth century as local mutual organisations. Home ownership would not have spread so widely in Great Britain without the financial mechanisms which they have provided. Their dominant role in financing home ownership is probably unique among countries where home ownership is the largest tenure, and places their operations at the centre of housing policy. This poses the question of whether Government should take power to exert greater influence over building societies' borrowing and lending practices.

7.06 The Government would prefer to work on the basis of voluntary co-operation with the societies. The societies have in recent years co-operated with each other, and with local authorities and the Government, in stabilising the flow of mortgage funds, lending further 'down market' on older houses and to people with lower incomes, and providing 'support' lending to make up for reductions in local authority lending. Whilst building societies must certainly satisfy themselves about the security of the funds invested with them, the Government consider that they could without risk go further in supporting the objectives of the national housing policy and that they should do so.

---

*Building societies do not in general subdivide their figures geographically, so the totals are United Kingdom totals. The figures in Chapter 7 therefore refer to the United Kingdom as a whole unless otherwise stated.

7.07 Local authorities have been a significant though relatively small source of mortgage funds. Their contribution has been especially valuable in inner city areas. A higher proportion of their lending than that of building societies has normally been directed to first-time house-buyers with lower incomes, and to older property. But local authorities will have an even more important task in providing a framework, through their local housing strategies and local plans, within which building societies can play their part.

7.08 There are two main obstacles which lie in the path of the steady growth of home ownership in the years ahead.

7.09 The first is the terms on which mortgages are made available. It would be unrealistic to believe that home ownership could be opened up to all; and it would be no kindness to tempt into the financial responsibilities of home ownership those who simply would not manage the mortgage payments. And there are those who, although they could afford home ownership, prefer to rent. They should have the choice. But there are probably a lot of people who want to become home owners, but whose needs do not quite fit into the conventional pattern of mortgage facilities and lending criteria applied across building society counters.

7.10 The second obstacle is the supply of mortgage funds. The demand for new mortgages each year is now very great—the number granted in recent years has averaged some 700,000 a year, comprising 400,000 first-time buyers and 300,000 subsequent buyers. These numbers will rise, but only if matched by adequate mortgage funds.

7.11 The rest of this chapter considers these and other related issues under the headings:

—House purchase—with special reference to the first-time house-buyer;

—The supply of mortgage funds;

—The supply of houses for sale.

HOUSE PURCHASE

7.12 In recent years about 50–60 per cent of all mortgages from the main lending institutions have gone to first-time purchasers. At current rates of tax relief, the gross interest payments by mortgagors eligible for relief at the basic rate are effectively reduced by about one-third.

7.13 About one-fifth of new mortgages in 1976 were endowment mortgages, on which interest only is paid each year, the capital being paid when a linked life insurance policy matures. But as explained in paragraph 4.09, most new mortgages take the form of 'annuity' loans, with a generally constant level of *gross* annual payments throughout the duration of the mortgage (unless mortgage interest rates change), whether tax relief or option mortgage subsidy is claimed. When the annuity mortgage attracts tax relief, the annual *net* payments rise year by year. This is because the proportion of the gross payment attributable

51

to interest reduces each year—and so therefore does the amount of tax relief—as the capital debt is paid off. The position is different with option mortgage subsidy, under which a purchaser may choose to pay a subsidised mortgage interest rate and does not receive tax relief. The lender reclaims the subsidy from the Government. To the purchaser, the value of the subsidy is roughly equivalent to tax relief on mortgage interest at the basic rate. But these annual subsidised payments, unlike the net payments on a tax relief mortgage, remain constant (unless mortgage interest rates change). This is because the option mortgage is calculated at an annuity rate net of subsidy (see Figure 9).

7.14 The typical mortgagor can expect the real burden of annual net payments to decline over time—whether he opts for tax relief or subsidy—as his income rises. But the initial annual payments can be heavy for a first-time buyer who borrows as much as he can in relation to his income—often well over 20 per cent of post-tax income, especially when interest rates are relatively high (see Figure 10 and the discussion of interest rates in Chapter 4). And some people who want to own their own home find that they fall just short of current requirements for a mortgage. Their present income may be slightly too low. They may not be able to raise a large enough initial deposit. They may want to buy an older house, often in need of renovation or repair and sometimes in a run-down locality.

7.15 The Government have therefore concentrated attention on schemes which would ease financial burdens in the early years and thereby help into home ownership people who might not quite have been able to buy otherwise, and also help those who might have bought anyway, though with great difficulty.

Flexibility in Building Society Lending

7.16 The problems of many potential first-time purchasers with modest incomes could be eased if building societies were more able and ready:

—to provide low-start mortgages, easing the burden in the early years;

—to offer higher percentage mortgages for those who cannot raise a sufficient deposit;

—to extend further their lending on older property, especially in inner urban areas.

7.17 *Low-start mortgages.* Payments on a low-start mortgage are lower initially but higher subsequently than those on a conventional annuity mortgage. Low-start mortgage schemes are a means of partially offsetting the high real cost of mortgage payments in early years (see discussion of front loading, interest rates and inflation in Chapter 4). Two national low-start mortgage schemes have been devised—one by the National Economic Development Office and one by the Depaitment of the Environment in conjunction with the Building Societies Association (BSA). Both provide for a gradual annual rise in payments from the initial low-start. Figure 11 compares the profile of periodic payments under the DOE/BSA low-start scheme and the NEDO scheme with that under a conventional annuity mortgage, all net of option mortgage subsidy.

7.18 It would be unwise of course for lenders to provide—and for borrowers to enter into—low-start mortgage facilities which in later years lead to very sharp increases in annual payments in relation to income, caused by too large a build-up of outstanding debt. Consequently the rate of rise of scheduled payments needs to be set so as to provide a safety margin to allow for increases in mortgage interest rates, and for the mortgagor's income not keeping up with prices—either because incomes in general for a time rise more slowly than prices, or because the individual mortgagor's income lags behind the general increase. The progression of payments under the schemes illustrated in Figure 12 seems to provide a reasonably adequate safety margin. For a mortgagor whose income grew, but less than prices increased, the burden would fall more slowly; but it would still fall.

7.19   There is no way of knowing how large the potential demand for low-start mortgages may be. But there clearly is a considerable potential demand from a substantial minority of people with modest incomes who want to become home owners. Just over one-tenth of all local authority mortgages issued in 1975 were low-start mortgages, but building societies have issued few so far.

7.20   A low-start mortgage might not be attractive to people buying their first house who could afford higher initial outgoings—for example, a newly married couple without children and both at work. But for some potential purchasers low-start mortgages could be particularly welcome—for example a couple with children and only one earner, with an income which is modest but likely to rise by promotion or on the wife's return to work. And, because of the lower initial payments, lenders might reasonably make larger loans than the potential borrower's income would otherwise attract.

7.21   Low-start mortgages could be particularly useful for house-buyers who choose an option mortgage rather than claiming tax relief on mortgage interest, because the initial payments under the option mortgage scheme are higher than those under a comparable tax relief mortgage (see Figure 9)—about 9 per cent higher in the first year, if the interest rate is 11 per cent and the basic rate of tax is 35 per cent. This characteristic of option mortgage subsidy could be offset if the payments were calculated on the basis of a low-start mortgage.

7.22   The Government hope that building societies will make low-start mortgages more widely available and, in particular, offer the choice of a low-start mortgage to those borrowers who select the option mortgage subsidy in preference to tax relief on interest.

7.23   Since low-start mortgages involve lower repayments of principal in the early years, lenders need additional capital inflows if the level of new lending is to be sustained. Low-start mortgages are also more complicated for lenders to administer than conventional forms of mortgage. But the slower repayment of principal should not prove an insuperable barrier to wider provision of such mortgages as they would be only a minority of all advances. And administratively simpler forms of low-start mortgage with different repayment profiles may be devised.

7.24   A very different form of low-start is provided by equity sharing schemes, which fall somewhere between owning and renting. An example is the 'half and

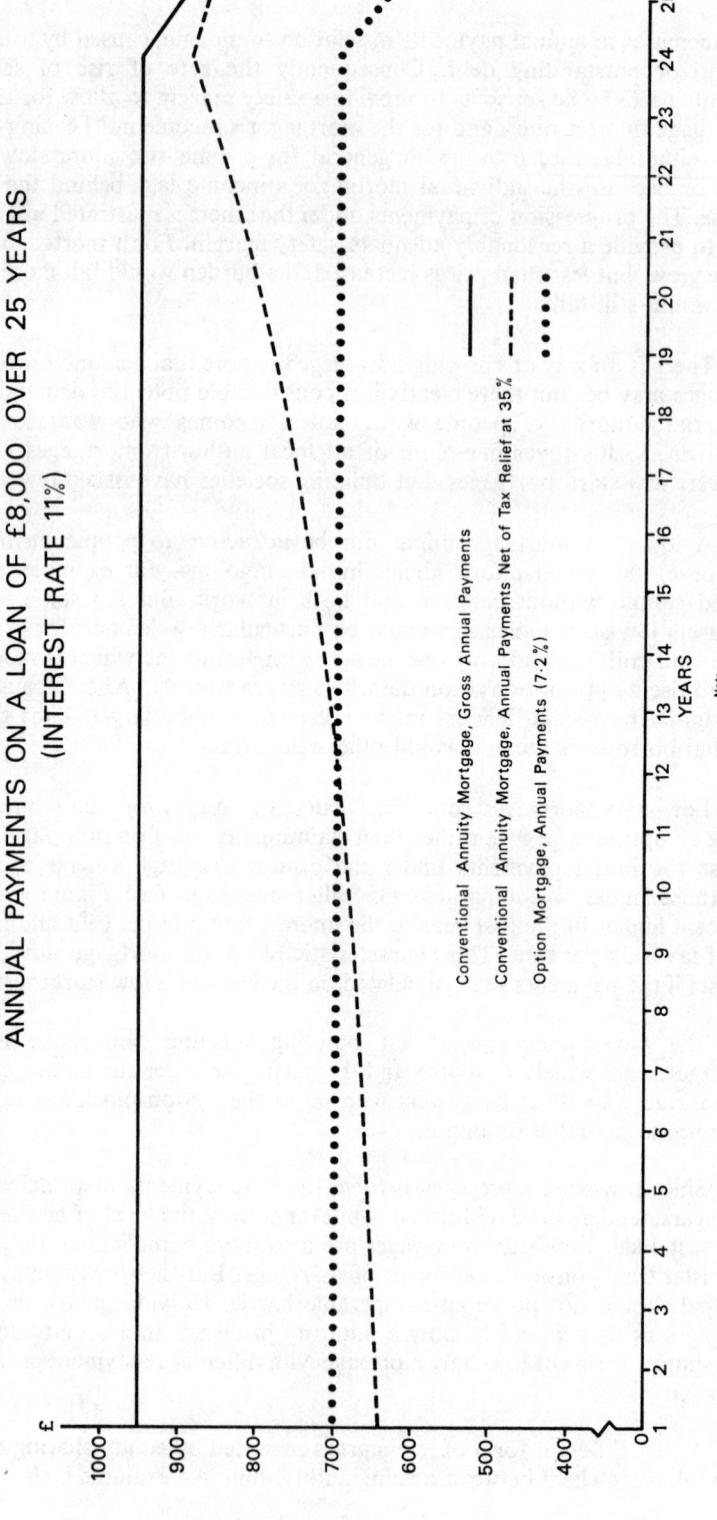

Figure 9: THE CONVENTIONAL ANNUITY MORTGAGE AND THE OPTION MORTGAGE COMPARED :
ANNUAL PAYMENTS ON A LOAN OF £8,000 OVER 25 YEARS
(INTEREST RATE 11%)

Conventional Annuity Mortgage, Gross Annual Payments

Conventional Annuity Mortgage, Annual Payments Net of Tax Relief at 35%

Option Mortgage, Annual Payments (7.2%)

YEARS

Note

Monthly payments cease immediately the principal has been repaid during the last year of the term. This generally leads to a lower annual payment in that year.

54

Figure 10: REAL BURDEN OF PAYMENTS IMPOSED BY A CONVENTIONAL ANNUITY MORTGAGE WITH TAX RELIEF OR WITH OPTION MORTGAGE SUBSIDY

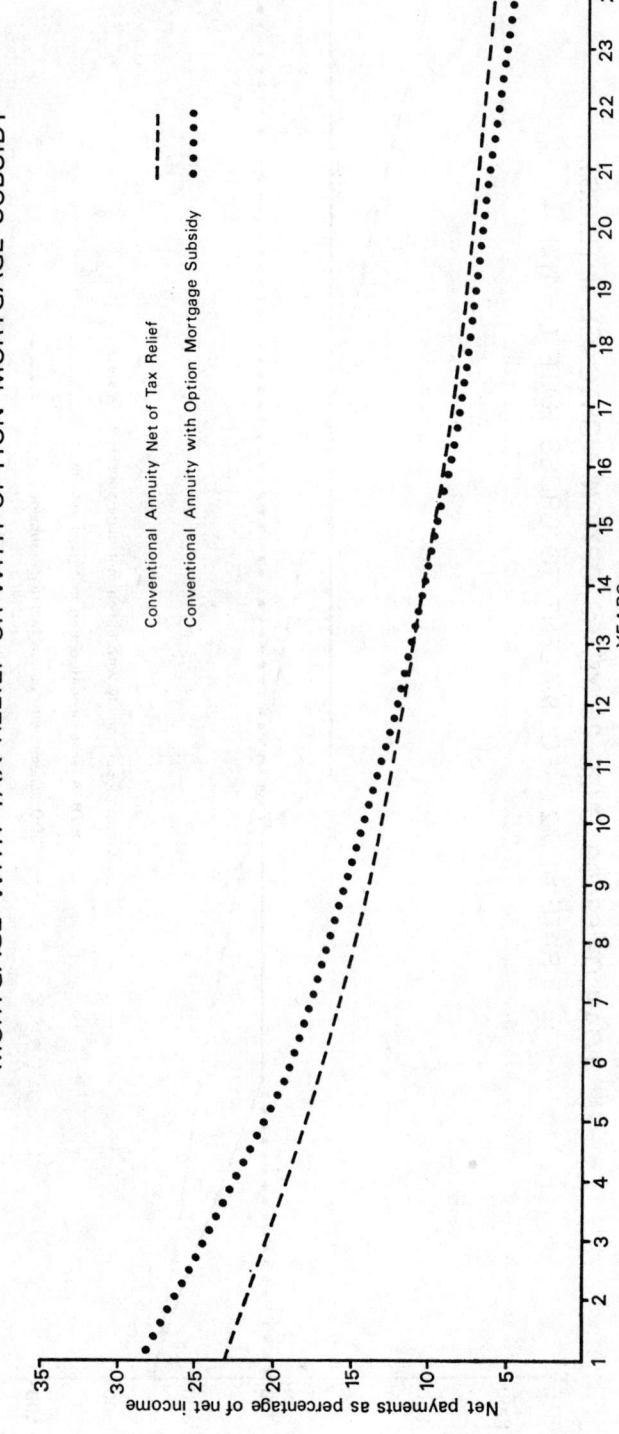

Conventional Annuity Net of Tax Relief

Conventional Annuity with Option Mortgage Subsidy

Net payments as percentage of net income

YEARS

Assumptions: Loan of £8,000 over 25 years at 11% (option mortgage rate 7·2%). Loan is 2 1/2 times gross annual income in first year; gross income rises at 8% pa thereafter; personal tax reliefs rise at 8% pa from 1976/77 levels.

55

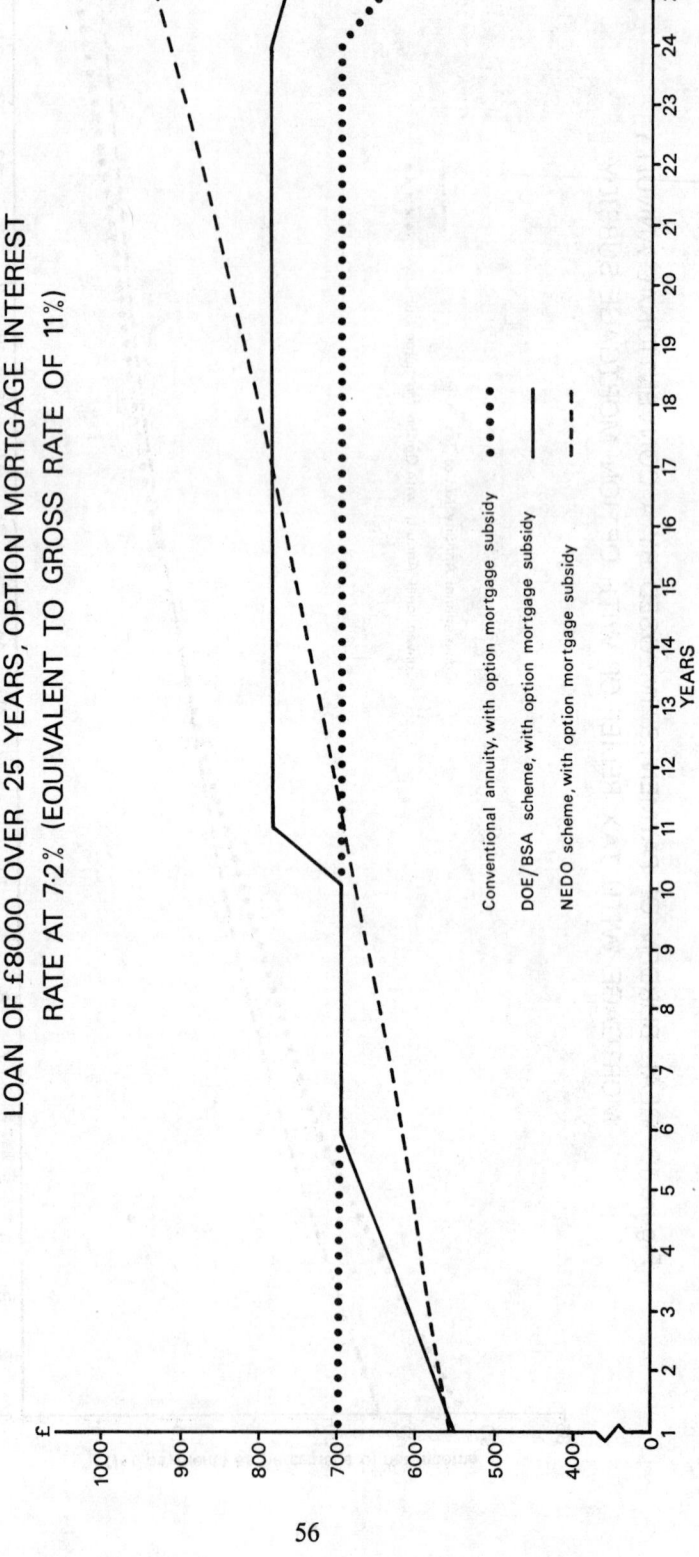

Figure 11: TWO NATIONAL LOW-START SCHEMES COMPARED WITH A CONVENTIONAL ANNUITY WITH OPTION MORTGAGE SUBSIDY: ANNUAL PAYMENTS ON A LOAN OF £8000 OVER 25 YEARS, OPTION MORTGAGE INTEREST RATE AT 7·2% (EQUIVALENT TO GROSS RATE OF 11%)

• • • • • Conventional annuity, with option mortgage subsidy

——— DOE/BSA scheme, with option mortgage subsidy

– – – NEDO scheme, with option mortgage subsidy

YEARS

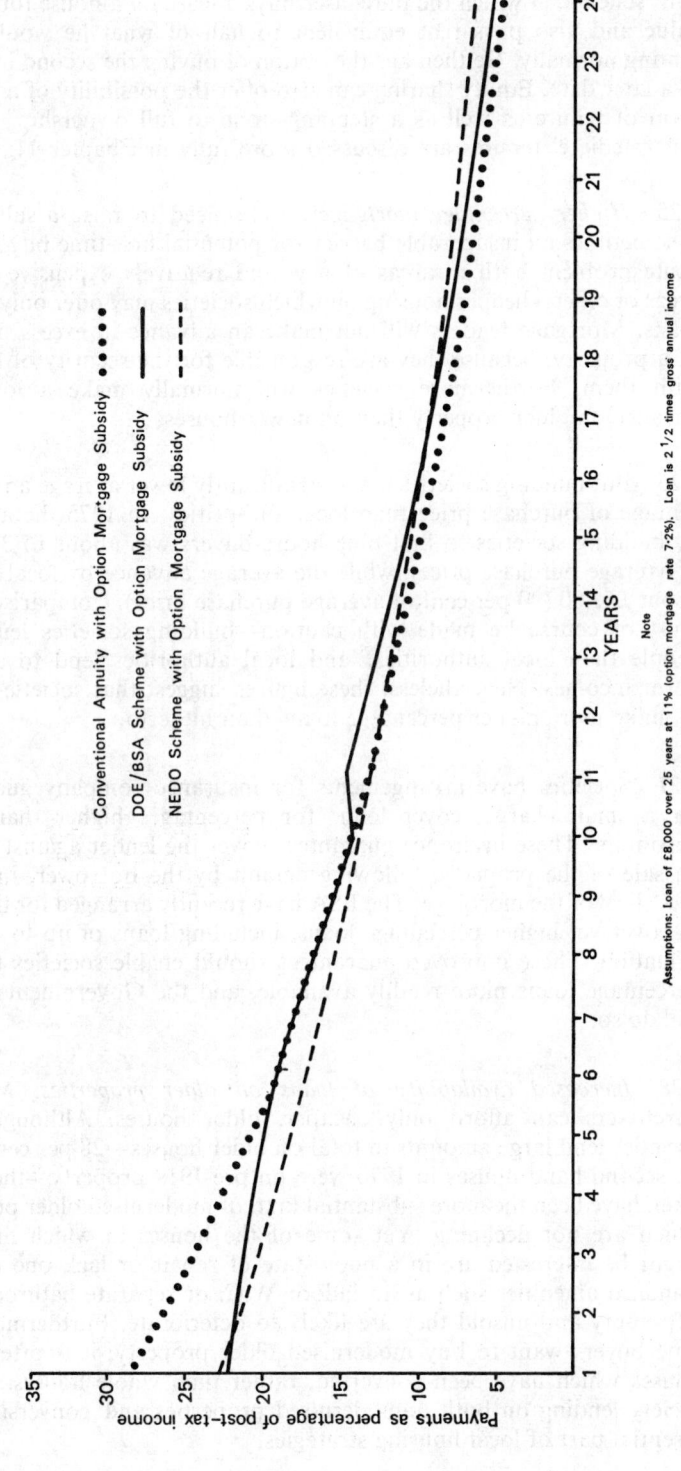

Figure 12 : REAL BURDEN OF PAYMENTS IMPOSED BY A CONVENTIONAL ANNUITY
MORTGAGE AND BY THE TWO NATIONAL LOW-START SCHEMES

•••• Conventional Annuity with Option Mortgage Subsidy

—— DOE/BSA Scheme with Option Mortgage Subsidy

– – – NEDO Scheme with Option Mortgage Subsidy

Note

Assumptions: Loan of £8,000 over 25 years at 11% (option mortgage rate 7-2%). Loan is 2 1/2 times gross annual income
in first year; gross income rises at 8% pa thereafter; personal tax reliefs rise at 8% pa from 1976/77 levels.

Payments as percentage of post-tax income

YEARS

57

half' scheme, in which the purchaser buys a lease on a house for half its market value and also pays rent equivalent to half of what he would pay were he renting normally. He then has the option of buying the second half of the house at a later date. Equity sharing can also offer the possibility of a new permanent form of tenure as well as a stepping-stone to full ownership. This and other 'intermediate' tenures are discussed more fully in Chapter 11.

7.25 *Higher percentage mortgages.* The need to raise a substantial deposit is sometimes an insuperable barrier for potential first-time buyers. It can be an acute problem both in areas of new and relatively expensive houses, and in areas of older, cheaper housing on which societies may offer only low percentage loans. Mortgage lenders will not make an advance in excess of the valuation of a property, because they are responsible for the security of the funds saved with them. Furthermore societies will normally make a lower percentage advance on older property than on newer houses.

7.26 But building societies make significantly lower average advances as a percentage of purchase price than local authorities. In 1975 the average advance by building societies to first-time house-buyers was about £7,300 (76 per cent of average purchase price), while the average advance by local authorities was about £6,400 (90 per cent of average purchase price). Comparisons such as this must of course be made with caution—building societies lend to far more people than local authorities, and local authorities lend to applicants with lower incomes. Nevertheless, these figures suggest that societies might be able to make more higher percentage loans than hitherto.

7.27 Societies have arrangements for insurance company guarantees which, for a small charge, cover loans for percentages higher than their normal maximum. These insurance guarantees cover the lender against the risk of loss on sale of the property, following default by the borrower, in respect of the top 'slice' of the mortgage. The BSA have recently arranged for these guarantees to cover yet higher percentage loans, including loans of up to 100 per cent of valuation. These improved guarantees should enable societies to make higher percentage loans more readily available, and the Government hope that they will do so.

7.28 *Increased availability of loans on older properties.* Many first-time purchasers can afford only cheaper, older houses. Although the building societies lend large amounts in total on older houses—28 per cent of their loans on second-hand houses in 1976 were on pre-1919 property—these houses may often have been the more substantial kind of modernised older property in areas which are not declining. Yet some of the houses in which first-time buyers might be interested are in a poor state of repair or lack one or more of the standard amenities such as an indoor W.C. or separate bathroom. If they are left empty and unsold they are likely to deteriorate. Furthermore, when first-time buyers want to buy modernised older property, it is often flats in large houses which have been converted, rather than whole houses. More building society lending on both unmodernised properties and conversions will be an essential part of local housing strategies.

Local co-operation between Building Societies and Local Authorities

7.29 The problems facing first-time buyers vary greatly from area to area. There is no single solution. The right answers can only be worked out through co-operation between building societies and local authorities at local level. The arrangements made in the last few years for support lending have provided a foundation on which effective working partnerships between them can be developed.

7.30 Building societies and local authorities should ensure that a wide range of mortgage facilities is provided, including low-start mortgages, higher percentage loans and more loans on older properties. Building societies are likely to remain the principal source of mortgage funds, but local authorities could complement their work especially in areas of older houses by providing:

—topping-up loans to the mortgagor to supplement a first loan from a building society;

—improvement or repair grants (see Chapter 10) to improve the security of building society loans;

—guarantees to societies that older properties are acceptable security for loans.

Legislation may be necessary to clarify and strengthen the powers of local authorities to make topping-up loans and to give guarantees.

7.31 In addition to complementing building society lending, local authorities must keep building societies fully informed of the development of their local housing strategies in general and of their plans for specific areas in particular. This will give building societies a sounder basis for assessing older properties as security for loans.

7.32 Such co-operation should help to ensure increased lending on houses which are old or in a poor state of repair. It should also help to reduce 'red-lining'—the withdrawal by societies of mortgage lending from declining areas at present seen as poor security for their funds and perhaps as poor investments for the house-buyers themselves. Building societies and local authorities, by working together at the local level, can assist in revitalising older urban areas including inner city areas. The expansion of home ownership in these areas will help retain younger people and encourage skilled people to come back.

Special Government Assistance for First-time Purchasers

7.33 Many first-time house-buyers would benefit from the developments proposed above, but it may take some years for their full potential to be realised. More needs to be done.

7.34 Some submissions to the Review have proposed additional Government help for first-time house-buyers in the form of continuing extra subsidies, covering the amount by which mortgage outgoings exceed a specified proportion of income. This would be an open-ended form of support. It would be highly

59

complex administratively, and involve periodic tests of income. The Government instead favour additional assistance in the early years for people who, after that, will be able to support house purchase by themselves.

7.35 The Government therefore propose to introduce special 'savings bonus and loans' schemes, for which legislation will be necessary. The details need to be worked out, but the schemes might consist of:

—Government savings bonus: all first-time house-buyers would be eligible for a bonus from the Government. It might be broadly equivalent to income tax at the basic rate on the aggregate of interest on up to £1000 of savings in the scheme, irrespective of liability to tax. The bonus would be available at the time of house purchase.

—Government loan: a £500 loan would be available to each first-time buyer who had saved at least a matching sum under the savings bonus scheme, had been saving for not less than 2 years, and who was buying a house within a specified house price limit (with variations by geographical area); the loan would be interest-free for the first 5 years and repayable with subsequent interest over the remaining duration of the mortgage or upon redemption of that mortgage.

If two or more people were buying jointly, their savings (taken together) would be eligible for only one bonus, and only one £500 loan could be claimed.

7.36 The *savings bonus* would provide an extra incentive to saving for house purchase, especially for those who need a longish period of time to save a substantial sum. For example, at an interest rate of 7 per cent net of tax at the basic rate:

—a couple putting aside £20 a month between them in a normal savings account with a building society would save over £1,000 after 5 years, and earn a Government bonus of about £100, on top of £260 normal interest net of tax;

—the same couple, putting aside £40 a month, would save £1,000 in just over two years, and would earn a bonus of about £30 on top of normal interest of about £75 net of tax;

—if they then stopped saving, but left the £1,000 in for another 2 years or so, the bonus would accumulate to £100, again on top of £260 normal interest net of tax.

7.37 The *loan* would help both those who are unable to buy because they cannot raise sufficient deposit, and those whose problem is the burden of payments in the early years. The latter would be able to take a smaller mortgage than otherwise, or might perhaps use the loan to meet part of the payments in the early years (see Figure 13); both methods would effectively provide a low-start mortgage. The waiver of interest for the first five years on the £500 Government loan would be worth £200 (at an interest rate of 7 per cent net of tax at the basic rate).

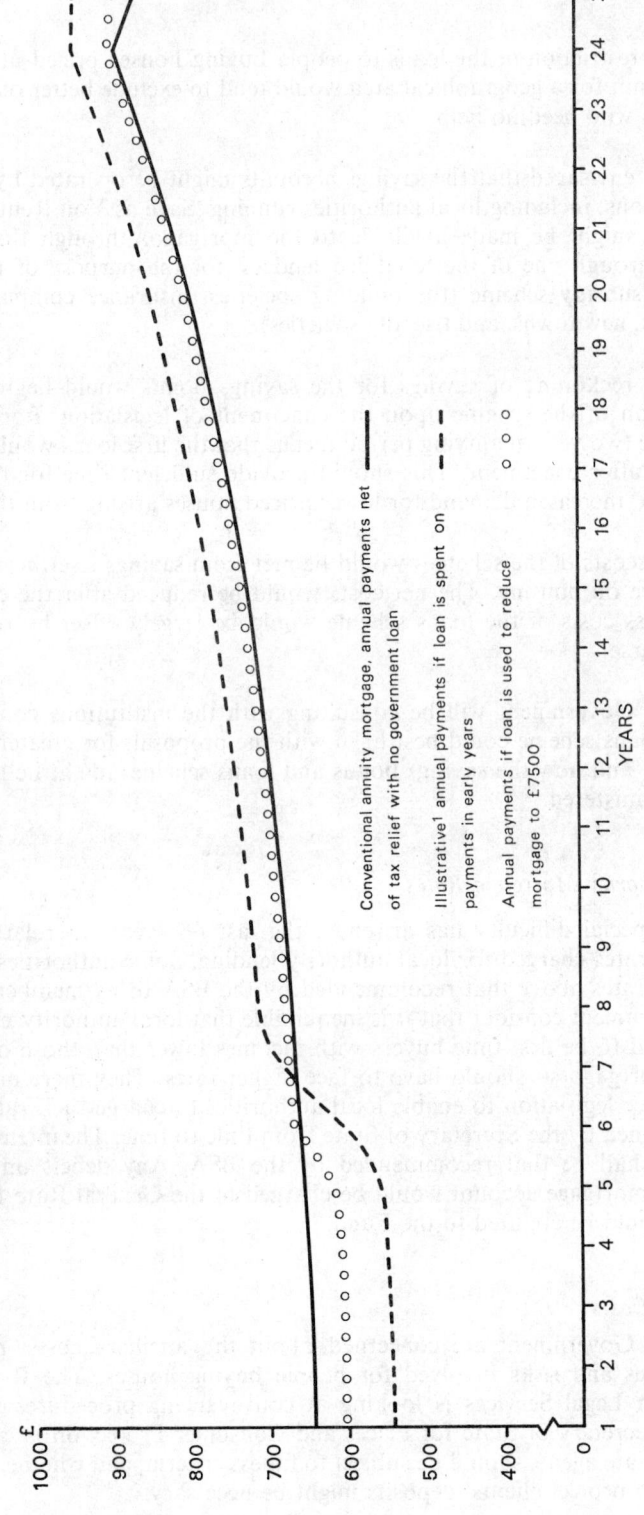

Figure 13: EFFECTS OF A £500 GOVERNMENT LOAN INTEREST FREE FOR FIRST FIVE YEARS ON ANNUAL PAYMENTS ON A LOAN OF £8000 OVER 25 YEARS AT 11%

Conventional annuity mortgage, annual payments net of tax relief with no government loan

Illustrative1 annual payments if loan is spent on payments in early years

Annual payments if loan is used to reduce mortgage to £7500

YEARS

1 It is assumed that the loan is spent in instalments of £50 at the end of each half-year, and that the remaining sum held by the mortgagor earns interest at 7%

7.38 The restriction of the loans to people buying houses priced at not more than the limit for a geographical area would tend to exclude better off first-time purchasers who need no help.

7.39 It is envisaged that the savings accounts might be operated by a variety of institutions, including local authorities running 'Save as You Rent' schemes. The loans might be made available to the mortgagor through the lender— perhaps through one of the 'qualified lenders' for the purpose of the option mortgage subsidy scheme (the building societies, insurance companies, local authorities, new towns, and friendly societies).

7.40 The reckoning of savings for the savings bonus would begin with the introduction of the scheme upon the enactment of legislation. For the loans scheme the two year qualifying period means that the first loans would be made two years after enactment. This should provide sufficient time for the market to adjust to increased demand for lower priced houses arising from the scheme.

7.41 The costs of the schemes would be met from savings elsewhere in public expenditure on housing. The net costs would be reduced after the early years as the gross costs of the loans scheme would be largely offset by repayments in due course.

7.42 The Government will be consulting with the institutions concerned on how the loans scheme could best fit in with the proposals for greater flexibility in lending, and how the savings bonus and loans schemes might be most effectively administered.

Local Authority Mortgage Rates

7.43 A special difficulty has arisen in the last few years in relation to the mortgage rates charged for local authority lending. Some authorities have had to charge rates above that recommended by the BSA to its member societies. The Government consider that it is inequitable that local authority mortgagors —who tend to be first-time buyers with incomes lower than those of building society mortgagors—should have to face higher rates. They therefore propose to introduce legislation to enable local authorities to charge such rates as may be determined by the Secretary of State from time to time. The intention is that this rate shall be that recommended by the BSA. Any deficit on the local authority mortgage account would be charged to the General Rate Fund; any surplus would be credited to the Fund.

Ancillary Costs

7.44 The Government are concerned about the ancillary costs, procedural complexities and risks involved for people buying houses. The Royal Commission on Legal Services is looking at conveyancing procedures and costs. And the Secretary of State for Prices and Consumer Protection is considering whether estate agents should be subject to fitness criteria, and whether measures designed to protect clients' deposits might be necessary.

Implementation

7.45 We cannot say exactly what response there might be to the measures to widen access to home ownership. But it is reasonable to expect that the number of extra first-time buyers might run into tens of thousands a year, over and above those who were helped to buy sooner than they could otherwise have done. Some of these measures will also help existing home owners who want to move and buy another house.

7.46 Measures to widen access to home ownership will increase the number of applications for mortgages from people with modest incomes and from those who may want to buy cheaper, older houses. This does not mean that building societies should allow social judgement to supersede commercial judgement. The Government do not intend that any of the proposals to widen entry into home ownership should lead societies into irresponsible investment of personal savings entrusted to them. That would be quite wrong. But within the limits of acceptable and reasonable commercial risk, societies ought to give due weight to social factors when deciding what priority to give to applications for mortgages. The measures discussed below to secure a reasonably stable supply of mortgage funds should help by avoiding the very long queues for mortgages that formed in past mortgage famines. But whether the queue is long or short, the borrower with a modest income or the borrower who wants to buy a border-line house should not on that account alone be more likely to have to go to the back of the queue, and stay there longer, than other would-be house-buyers.

7.47 This will admittedly involve building societies in troublesome judgements on priorities in dealing with mortgage applications from classes of potential borrowers and from individuals. But these difficulties are not insoluble. Some societies have already earned for themselves a well-deserved reputation for socially responsible lending policies.

SUPPLY OF MORTGAGE FUNDS

7.48 The growth of home ownership makes the supply of mortgage funds a matter of ever increasing importance. There are two principal issues:

—how to secure a reasonably stable flow of mortgage funds, in the interests of first-time house purchasers, existing home owners who want to move, and the house-building industry;

—how to secure a growth in the supply of mortgage funds sufficient to meet an increasing demand.

A Stable Supply of Mortgage Funds

7.49 The flow of funds available to building societies for making loans comprises repayments of principal by mortgagors, interest due to investors that is credited to their accounts instead of being paid out to them, and the excess of new money invested over withdrawals (net receipts). The first two are comparatively stable, but net receipts fluctuate widely.

7.50 As indicated in Chapter 4, building societies' net receipts from investors have proved very sensitive to changes in the balance between the interest rates offered by them and by their competitors. These competing rates have fluctuated sharply in recent years—by as much as 4 per cent in 3 months. Building societies cannot match such oscillations. They can alter the rates offered to investors virtually overnight, but to increase the interest rate on some $4\frac{1}{2}$ million building society mortgages is a major administrative task, especially as under many (particularly older) mortgage deeds, 1–3 months' notice of an increase must be given. This lag adds to the cost to societies of raising their rate structure. Moreover, when building societies raise their rates to investors because competing rates have risen, the enhanced rate is paid on all money invested with them, not just the money on the margin that might be attracted to competitors. This means, for example, that to match a 4 per cent increase in market interest rates would require an increase of 2·6 per cent in the (tax paid) rate payable on all invested money, at a cost of nearly £950m a year. This increase in interest costs would have to be recouped by a $4\frac{1}{4}$–$4\frac{1}{2}$ per cent increase in the mortgage interest rate.

7.51 An increase of this order would be self-defeating. It would secure an increase in the supply of mortgage funds, but at the expense of imposing great strains on the household budgets of existing mortgagors and putting the price of a new mortgage beyond the reach of many potential first-time house-buyers. Even the need for a smaller increase however can put societies into a difficult position. The natural concern of those existing mortgagors who do not want to move is that mortgage rates should not go up. The equally natural concern of many potential first-time buyers and of existing home owners who also want to move is that there should be enough mortgage funds to go round, even if this means a general increase in mortgage rates.

7.52 The combination of the reluctance of societies to alter their interest rates substantially or frequently, and of volatile interest rates in the economy as a whole, has led to large variations in building societies' receipts, and consequently in alternating mortgage 'feasts' and 'famines' damaging to house-buyers, home owners, and house-builders.

7.53 The Government attach great importance to measures to mitigate the effects of swings in the general level of interest rates on the supply of mortgage funds, although it clearly would be unrealistic to try to insulate the housing market completely from external economic events. Good progress has already been made by the Joint Advisory Committee on Building Society Mortgage Finance (JAC), the body established in October 1973 for consultation between the Government departments and the BSA. Under a memorandum agreed in April 1975, the building societies when taking in a substantial inflow of receipts after competing rates have fallen do not necessarily increase their lending to the maximum possible extent or reduce their interest rates to cut back the inflow, but instead build up their liquid funds. These funds can then be drawn on to keep up lending when competing rates rise and net receipts fall back. This procedure smooths out peaks and troughs in mortgage lending.

7.54 There were no effective stabilisation arrangements in force in time to avert the mortgage 'famine' of 1973/74, which was ended in 1974 by the

Government's £500m short term loan, followed by a fall in competing interest rates. This fall continued during 1975 and the early months of 1976, enabling building societies to build up liquidity to about 22 per cent (seasonally adjusted) of total assets by the spring of 1976. This was about 6–7 per cent above the level which societies generally regard as normal for operating purposes. The extra 6–7 per cent comprised some £1,500–1,750m of liquid funds, sufficient to finance some 200,000–230,000 mortgage advances (including those financed from relending loans redeemed on sale of mortgaged houses). There was a sharp rise in competing rates of interest in the spring of 1976. But the large margin of liquid funds enabled the building societies—without a compensating increase in their own rate structure until the general level of interest rates rose again later in the year—to avoid a severe reduction in their lending in the second half of 1976. The building societies maintained new mortgage commitments at a rate of £500m in the second half of the year—less than £20m lower than in the first half—by the reduction of liquidity to 18 per cent of total assets by the end of 1976.

7.55 The Government believe that an even greater degree of stability can be achieved by developing the voluntary arrangements with the building societies through the JAC. They consider that building societies should:

(a) plan to build up stabilisation 'funds' when competing interest rates move in their favour to amounts greater than the 6–7 per cent of assets achieved in the spring of 1976;

(b) keep their structure of rates paid to investors more in line with the market, so that there is less fluctuation in the inflow of funds into the societies;

(c) adopt a more flexible relationship between the rate paid by mortgagors and the rate paid to investors, by varying the latter more frequently or to a greater extent or both. This would avoid disturbing the household budgets of mortgagors more often than absolutely necessary, and would avoid the costs of frequent changes in mortgage rates. It would mean that on occasion mortgagors would pay slightly higher rates and investors receive slightly lower rates (with societies appearing to make 'profits' as compared with a situation where the two rates moved strictly together); and on occasion mortgagors would pay lower and investors receive higher rates (with societies appearing to make 'losses'). Neither mortgagors nor investors would lose, taking one year with another;

(d) be prepared to raise short-term loans on the money market to replace funds from normal sources lost when the general level of interest rates rises suddenly. Such short-term loans need form only a very small proportion of the total funding of building societies. It is common financial practice for large investments to attract higher interest rates. Whilst building societies would therefore have to pay higher rates than those paid to conventional investors, the total cost would be much lower than that of raising the equivalent sum by increasing the rates paid to investors generally (see paragraph 7.50). The effect on the mortgage rate would be correspondingly smaller.

7.56   The Government believe that the societies have both the capacity and the will to operate such arrangements, but would consider helping in two ways:

(a) Building up stabilisation funds could, at times, involve societies in making a loss, since they might be paying more to their investors than they could get by reinvesting these funds in the money market. The Government might accept part of the funds for investment in the National Loans Fund at an interest rate which would not involve the societies in a loss, subject to agreement through the JAC on the size of mortgage lending and of stabilisation funds.

(b) The Government would be prepared, in exceptional circumstances, to consider providing short-term loans from public funds as in 1974. But instances where such loans might be needed should be very rare if the arrangements described above were applied effectively.

An Adequate Supply of Mortgage Funds

7.57   Building society lending has grown and will continue to grow (see paragraph 4.20). The growth will be increased further by the steps suggested above to widen access to home ownership.

7.58   On present trends and prospects, the number of advances to be made by building societies could rise from 651,000 in 1975 and 715,000 in 1976 to 800,000 a year at the beginning of the nineteen eighties and 900,000 a year by the middle of the decade, allowing for increased demand following the measures to assist first-time house-buyers set out earlier in this chapter.

7.59   Building societies have of late taken in about £1,000m-£1,200m a year in 'small' savings of less than £500, with the rest coming in larger amounts. The small savings might rise in line with incomes. But that would leave a substantial amount to be raised from larger investments by individuals on building societies' normal terms, or from new sources.

7.60   It may be that all the funds that will be needed will be found from building societies' present sources—personal savings (often liable to withdrawal at short notice) held in ordinary, term, and subscription shares. In this connection it would help to spread available mortgage funds among more borrowers if all building societies were to extend the practice of requiring an existing mortgagor who moves to 'plough back' the net proceeds of sale into the purchase of the next house.

7.61   But there can be no certainty about financial flows some years ahead. It is, therefore, possible that the building societies will only be able to meet demands placed upon them for advances if they supplement their traditional sources of finance by raising funds from other financial institutions—in particular life and pension funds. The form of security would have to suit the investing institutions, and might be medium-term or long-term for the most part. This would be a supplementary source of finance, and funds raised from it would be for many years a small proportion of building societies' total liabilities. As with the proposal in paragraph 7.55(d), the effect on the level of mortgage rates would be very small.

7.62 If fresh sources of funds have to be tapped, building societies—especially the larger ones—might well both be able and prefer to deal direct with financial institutions. But the case for a special financial intermediary might be considered. This would raise funds from financial institutions and on-lend them to building societies. An intermediary, by virtue of its size, might be able to get better terms, with regard to interest rate and period of loan, than medium-sized and smaller societies acting independently. There could be savings in staff. Such an agency could also help with raising short-term loans to stabilise the flow of funds to societies (see paragraph 7.55(d)).

7.63 If there were to be an intermediary, it could be a private or a public body. If a private agency, it might be largely owned and controlled by the building societies themselves. The body might concentrate on lending money to societies on terms virtually identical to those on which it borrowed the money, in which case its need for capital (including both paid-up capital and reserves) and liquid assets would be relatively small. Alternatively, it might borrow on terms which suited the institutional lender and on-lend to societies on terms which more closely suited their requirements. In this latter case its needs for capital and liquid assets would be greater, because for example it would need to be able to absorb temporary differences between its borrowing and lending rates if market interest rates moved against it.

7.64 Another approach would be to establish the agency as a public body, with some direct Government participation. But this could clearly involve a greater degree of Government involvement in building society borrowing and lending policies. If an intermediary proves to be the best solution, the Government believe that the societies would themselves prefer to develop any necessary machinery.

SUPPLY OF HOUSES FOR SALE

7.65 Measures to ease access to house purchase and to secure a reasonably stable and sufficient supply of mortgage funds will clearly improve the house-building industry's prospects. Many of the new first-time buyers brought in by the measures discussed would buy second-hand houses. Some of these would be local authority or new town houses, some would be houses released from the private rented sector and some would be houses that, without these measures, might have been left empty to decay. But there will clearly also be some increased demand for new houses for sale—either directly from first-time buyers or from existing owners selling to first-time buyers.

7.66 For builders to be able to plan to meet the demand, they need as much assurance as possible that by the time the houses are ready—typically 6 to 12 months after starting—potential buyers will not be thwarted by shortage of mortgage funds. The private house-building industry suffered badly in the early nineteen seventies because of violent oscillations in the supply of funds. The degree of stabilisation already secured since 1974 has provided a steadier level of effective demand for new houses. The Government believe that the further development of arrangements to stabilise the flow of funds should enable builders to make forward plans with more confidence, and should also enable building societies to go further in providing advance mortgage 'quotas' for builders. Such arrangements do not involve lending direct to builders; quotas merely involve reserving funds for creditworthy purchasers to whom the builder can sell his houses.

7.67 In making their plans, builders also need to be reasonably sure that adequate land will be available on which to build. The duty placed on local authorities by the Community Land Act and the need to have regard to this in working out local housing strategies was emphasised in paragraph 6.07. Authorities will come to play an increasingly important role as suppliers of land to the industry as the Community Land Scheme develops. This linkage of a developing 'supply' role with the long-standing planning functions of authorities should help to provide a further element of stability for the industry, both in the flow of land on to the market and in the price at which it is obtainable.

CONCLUSION

7.68 The proposals outlined in this chapter will support and foster the growth of home ownership, and will benefit all those who want to own their own homes and can reasonably expect to do so in time.

7.69 Building societies occupy a pivotal position in the growth of home ownership as they supply most of the finance for house purchase. Greater emphasis on home ownership does not mean less social emphasis in housing policy. On the contrary, the widening of entry into home ownership for people with modest incomes will help to solve housing problems which used to be faced largely by the public sector, as well as satisfying deep-seated social aspirations. The building societies have already responded positively to Government initiatives by entering into voluntary arrangements to stabilise the flow of mortgage funds and to provide 'support' lending for local authorities. The Government hope and expect that the building societies will be ready to shoulder still greater responsibility and to extend their voluntary co-operation with central and local government in the expansion of home ownership within the framework of the national housing policy.

CHAPTER 8

Private Rented Housing

8.01 National statistics assign to the private rented sector all houses not owner-occupied and not let by local authorities or new town corporations—a total of 2·8 million. The term 'sector' may give the impression that the private rented sector is homogeneous. In fact there is such a variety of types of accommodation and terms of occupancy that no single policy towards private renting could be comprehensive.

THE MAKE-UP OF THE SECTOR

8.02 The three main divisions in the private rented sector are between:

—*conventional private tenancies:* about 2 million, of which about 1½ million are let unfurnished and about ½ million are let furnished;

—*lettings 'tied' to employment:* about 700,000, including a substantial number of lettings by public bodies, such as armed services married quarters; and

—*housing association tenancies:* over 200,000—although these are strictly part of the private sector, it is more convenient to consider them in the next chapter, as part of the public sector, in view of their social role.

These figures are for households and are approximate estimates of the current position, using the 1971 Census as a base. The total, 2·9 million, is somewhat higher than the total of houses given in paragraph 8.01 above, because many private tenants rent part of someone else's house.

8.03 Since the First World War there has been a statutory framework for the relationship of landlord and tenant in the private sector embodied in successive Rent Acts. The Acts deal both with security of tenure and maximum rents—two aspects of protection which are very closely linked. Current legislation, which governs the 2 million conventional private tenancies mentioned in paragraph 8.02 above, makes an important distinction between tenants of resident and non-resident private landlords.

—Tenants of non-resident landlords, and some established unfurnished tenants of resident landlords (in total about 1·8 million), generally enjoy full Rent Act protection. The majority of these (perhaps about 1·4 million) are 'regulated' tenants who are liable to pay 'fair rents' fixed by rent officers or, on objection, by rent assessment committees. A minority (somewhat less than 400,000) are controlled tenants whose rents are fixed in relation to 1956 gross rateable values and a proportion of the costs of certain subsequent repairs and improvements.

—Tenants of resident landlords (perhaps about 200,000) normally have only restricted protection under the Rent Acts. They can apply to rent tribunals to suspend notices to quit and to fix reasonable rents.

8.04 Many people in 'tied' accommodation are licensees paying only a nominal rent or no rent at all, and are not eligible for the full security available to tenants. But agricultural workers and their successors now enjoy equivalent protection as a result of the Rent (Agriculture) Act 1976.

8.05 Most private tenants fall into one or other of five main categories.

—Elderly people, often now with low incomes, who are regulated or controlled tenants of unfurnished accommodation. They may have lived in their present houses for many years. Similar people in younger age groups would normally become public sector tenants or home owners. When these tenants leave, the houses are often not re-let but are sold for home owner-ship, bought by local authorities or demolished.

—Older single people and couples without children who cannot afford home ownership. If not accepted for public sector tenancies they will need to rent privately on a long-term basis.

—Newly married couples, or young single people setting up home for the first time. Most of these will be private tenants for a short time only. In due course they will become home owners or public sector tenants. The National Movers Surveys of 1971 and 1973, commissioned by the Department of the Environment, showed a steady flow of such house-holds into private rented housing. A study of the housing experiences of newly married couples carried out for the Department of the Environment in 1975 showed that some 31 per cent of the couples interviewed were renting privately seven months after their marriage.

—People who move from one place to another to a new job or in order to train or study. This group includes immigrants from overseas. Few mobile households have ready access to public sector housing, even if they have previously occupied it elsewhere, and many cannot immediately become home owners. This is especially important in inner city areas which have traditionally been reception areas for such mobile people.

—Members of families who split up as a result of domestic difficulties often need quick access to furnished rented accommodation, which may only be available in the private sector.

8.06 It is not possible to estimate the size of these groups, but it is clear that most people in the first two categories occupy older houses under controlled or regulated unfurnished tenancies. There is little mobility in this part of the sector. The main problem is the poor physical state of the stock. The remaining categories of tenants are often in furnished flats and rooms in sub-divided properties, including lettings by resident landlords. Mobility is high. The main issue here is how much private rented housing will continue to be available in the foreseeable future for those who need it.

8.07 The geographical distribution of private rented accommodation is patchy. There are some private lettings in all areas, arising for example from sub-letting by home owners or public sector tenants or lettings by temporarily absent home owners. But the main concentration of private renting is in the inner cities and other urban areas first developed in the 19th century. It is a common characteristic of areas of housing stress or urban deprivation. The sector is particularly large in London. In 1971 some 25 per cent of all house-holds in England and Wales renting privately, and 37 per cent of all tenants in furnished accommodation, were to be found in London.

8.08 The 1976 English House Condition Survey showed that two-thirds of private rented houses were built before 1919. Roughly 15 per cent were statutorily unfit for human habitation, a further 15 per cent lacked one or more of the basic amenities and altogether about 33 per cent of the houses were in substantial disrepair. This is an improvement on the position in 1971 as regards basic amenities and unfitness, but the problem of disrepair has grown, as in other sectors (see Chapter 10).

THE DECLINE OF PRIVATE RENTING

8.09 The reduction in the proportion of the total stock comprising private rented housing—from something like 90 per cent before the First World War to about 15 per cent today—has already been briefly mentioned in Chapter 3. This has not arisen solely as a result of the growth of the other main sectors. The absolute numbers of private rented houses have also fallen. In 1938 there were 6·6 million; in 1960 4·6 million; there are now only 2·8 million.

8.10 Much of this reduction in the numbers of private rented houses need not give cause for concern. Many former tenants—or those who might once have become private tenants—have found more suitable long-term accommodation as home owners or public sector tenants. This process will continue, as the other sectors grow, and will be accentuated by measures such as the proposals for widening access to home ownership discussed in the previous chapter. But the needs of many of the people mentioned in paragraph 8·05 above will only be satisfactorily met by renting, and under present arrangements most of them would not have a very high priority in public sector waiting lists.

8.11 If the decline continued unabated and no action were taken to compensate for the loss of accommodation from the sector, many people—particularly new or mobile households—might not be able to find the housing they need. It might be argued—though the evidence is tenuous—that this is already beginning to happen in a number of areas. To guard against this, we need to consider what action can be taken to stimulate the supply of lettings within the private sector, and what can be done to provide accommodation in the public sector.

THE SCOPE FOR ACTION WITHIN THE SECTOR

8.12 Action within the private rented sector to compensate for the loss of accommodation and to prevent the decay of houses depends largely on what incentives landlords have to let their property, and to keep it in good repair.

8.13 It would be a mistake to think that all landlords are influenced by the same considerations. There are those who regard their property as a long-term investment providing a continuous income. These include companies, charitable bodies, and many private individuals who may own—by purchase or by inheritance—only one or two houses. But there are also owners who regard letting as a temporary means of making use of property for which they themselves have no immediate use. These include the home owner who lets his house while he is working abroad, the householder who lets spare rooms, and the owner of 'tied' accommodation which is not for the moment required for his workforce. In contrast with these, there are speculative landlords who have purchased blocks or estates of rented property with a view to realising their break-up value.

8.14 Landlords who see their property as a long-term investment tend to be mainly concerned with their net rental income. Landlords letting spare accommodation may be more concerned to be able to get possession when they need to do so rather than to secure the maximum rent. But it is difficult to generalise, and the Department of the Environment arranged for a major survey of the attitudes of existing landlords and tenants towards private renting to be carried out by the Office of Population Censuses and Surveys in the autumn of 1976. Results should be available later this year.

8.15 The nature of Government involvement in the private rented sector—based on statutory regulation—is quite different from that in the other main sectors. And the legislation itself is voluminous and complicated. For these reasons the problems of the private rented sector are being studied in detail in the separate Review of the Rents Acts. A consultation paper on the Review was issued on 31 January 1977 and comments were invited by 30 April. The Government's main conclusions should be announced by the end of the year. But it has been possible already to identify certain measures which could help to encourage improvement and repair of the privately rented housing stock and to stimulate the supply of accommodation for those who need quick access.

8.16 Some possibilities are outlined below. They do not alter the Government's commitment to the broad principle that private tenants of non-resident landlords should enjoy security of tenure, and that their rents should be restricted to reasonable levels. This is essential to prevent any recurrence of the exploitation and abuses which have so often appeared in the past when rented housing was not subject to the Rent Acts.

8.17 A central objective of policy for the private rented sector, as for other sectors, is that more sound older houses should be brought up to a decent standard and kept in good repair. The Government propose to modify the present system of improvement grants to encourage this, by making grants for repair work more readily available, and by making grants for basic amenities in multi-occupied property available as of right in appropriate cases. Consideration is being given to granting tenants the right to carry out improvements and to simplifying the procedures under which local authorities can require compulsory repairs. These proposals are discussed in more detail in Chapter 10.

8.18 Methods and criteria for fixing registered rents are being examined as a central issue in the Review of the Rent Acts. The outcome will have a bearing on the willingness of those landlords who see letting as a long-term investment to re-let accommodation when a vacancy occurs. Other measures for stimulating the supply of accommodation for those needing quick access are discussed below.

8.19 *Lettings by resident landlords.* Some accommodation is at present being held off the market by resident landlords and home owners who are temporarily absent from home. The problem is not so much rent levels as quick recovery of possession. Tenants of such landlords already normally have only restricted security, or are subject to provisions under which a court has no discretion to refuse an order for possession. Nevertheless, some home owners have faced difficulty and hardship in regaining possession, and reports of their experiences have promoted the idea that such lettings may be more trouble than they are worth.

8.20 The Government believe that there is a strong case for speeding up the procedures by which a resident landlord can regain possession from an unsatisfactory tenant. Under present provisions, no resident landlord who grants a proper weekly or monthly tenancy may evict his tenant without being liable to go to the rent tribunal, who may initially grant 6 months' suspension and further periods thereafter. Subsequently the landlord must obtain a court order for possession if the tenant does not leave of his own accord. The time-consuming nature of the whole process, and the uncertainties attendant on it, undoubtedly deter some potential resident landlords.

8.21 It would certainly be too far-reaching to abolish the need for a court order altogether, but there is a strong case for ending the role of the rent tribunal and for improving the procedure for obtaining a possession order. It would follow automatically that the present provision, under which a second fixed-term letting to a tenant of a resident landlord becomes fully protected, would disappear. It would be possible to amend the County Court Rules to provide a simplified procedure enabling a court hearing to take place within about 10 days in all cases where resident landlords or returning home owners had a mandatory right to repossession. Consideration is also being given to legislation which would provide for such cases to be heard by the registrar sitting in chambers rather than before the judge. These measures would help returning home owners to recover their homes more quickly.

8.22 *Flats over shops.* Accommodation normally let with a business is now frequently kept vacant if not needed by, say, the shop manager for the time being. If the accommodation is let separately it attracts full security of tenure and this may cause problems if the owner wishes to sell the business. Marginal changes to the Rent Acts could bring some of this accommodation back into use by putting it into the same category as a letting by a resident landlord, or making it subject to a mandatory order for possession.

8.23 *A new agency.* The two main reasons why new investment is not attracted to the private rented sector are undoubtedly the low rate of return from private renting, and the uncertainty about how changes in the statutory framework which might be made from time to time could affect the financial basis of investment. It seems possible that some institutional investors might be ready to finance marginal additions to the private rented sector, and to accept a modest real rate of return on capital, if they could be given assurances—in return for stipulated conditions of good management—about rent increases over the long term. The Government consider that it is worth investigating what terms

73

might attract new investment with a publicly accountable letting agency. Initial rents could be lower than initial costs of home ownership, but would be higher than rents for public sector housing. The market might therefore be largely confined to comparatively short-stay tenants, or working couples with quite high joint incomes, or single working people who shared accommodation. Nevertheless, this approach might result in useful additions to the housing stock.

ACTION IN OTHER SECTORS

8.24 It would be premature to reach conclusions about the longer-term future of private renting before the Review of the Rent Acts is completed. But it would not be easy to halt or reverse a process of contraction which has continued since the First World War. We cannot make an exact assessment of how further contraction of the private rented sector would affect people who have traditionally looked to it for housing, such as the categories of tenant listed in paragraph 8.05. But it is possible to draw some broad conclusions.

8.25 Some people in these groups—for example the frail elderly—can reasonably expect to receive a degree of priority in the allocation of public sector rented housing. Some may prefer to become home owners or to enter one of the newer forms of tenure; the opportunities to do so could be widened by the measures described in Chapters 7 and 11.

8.26 But many may not be able or may not want to become home owners, and yet their circumstances may be such that they would not normally be given priority in the allocation of public sector rented housing in 'pressure' areas where there are still formidable housing problems. These people will probably include young married couples, single working people, students, and those resident in an area only temporarily. Many of them will continue to look to the private rented sector for accommodation for some time to come. Measures proposed in paragraphs 8.12 to 8.23 to sustain the supply of private lettings should help to ease their problems, and further proposals may emerge from the Review of the Rent Acts. But it seems probable that the housing of such people will increasingly need to be taken into account in the development of local housing strategies and public sector allocation policies. This is discussed in the next chapter.

CHAPTER 9

The Public Sector

9.01 Every organisation involved in the provision of housing must share the social responsibility for seeing that the needs of the community are met within the framework provided by the Government's economic and financial policies. But public sector bodies—local authorities, new towns and housing associations —have a special part to play:

—Only the local authorities can take a comprehensive view of what should and can be done locally 'across the board' in both public and private sectors. Consequently it is for local authorities to assess the local housing situation as a whole, and keep it under regular review, through the local housing strategies discussed in Chapter 6, and through local plans;

—Local authorities, new towns and housing associations have a particular duty to provide for those who could not otherwise obtain a decent home. Local authorities—along with the other public sector bodies—must therefore provide housing which complements private sector provision so that the local stock is of satisfactory quality and matches the needs of the local population in terms of house size and type, location, and tenure.

This chapter looks primarily at the second of these functions—the public sector bodies as *providers* of housing.

9.02 Today, public sector authorities provide houses for roughly a third of all households in England and Wales. Their stock has grown from 2·2 million houses in 1951 to 5·5 million in 1976. In this period, 3·2 million new houses have been completed by local authorities, 0·2 million by new towns and 0·15 million by housing associations.

9.03 In addition to providing 'main-stream' housing for families with children the sector has dealt with many of the most serious housing problems, particularly through clearance and redevelopment of large areas of older cities. On occasion such redevelopment has gone too far. The social gain in providing new houses in this way has sometimes been less than the social loss involved in breaking up existing communities. We can learn a lot from the mistakes. But no-one should forget the horrors of the Victorian slums which the local authorities have now banished from most of our cities. The public sector has made a notable contribution towards raising the general level of housing conditions across the country.

9.04 Some public sector authorities have been steadily adapting their practices to meet new conditions. But the consistent development of local housing strategies within the framework of a national housing policy should enable all authorities to adjust their own activities more quickly and effectively in response to changing circumstances. Important trends which should be reflected in local strategies are:

—*The growth of the owner-occupied sector.* One of the consequences of the continuing growth and wider access to home ownership could be gradually

75

to narrow the social make-up of the public rented sector unless tenants can be offered more varied housing opportunities and a greater degree of personal independence and control over their homes.

—*The contraction of the private rented sector.* It seems likely that in the longer term the public sector must continue to take over many of the present functions of the private rented sector. This will involve some extension of the range of households for whom the public sector provides.

—*Demographic and social changes.* The marked growth in the number of small households will continue, particularly in the older age groups. The public sector has increasingly made provision for the elderly, especially in recent years. But the demand for public sector provision for them and for the disabled, and other groups who have difficulty in providing for themselves, will continue to grow.

9.05 Changes such as these will affect the pattern of public sector investment in housing and call for adjustments in management and allocation practices. This will often require difficult decisions to be taken on priorities in the light of the national housing policy and local needs as perceived by elected local representatives and the local community.

HOUSING INVESTMENT PROGRAMMES

9.06 We need much greater flexibility in the arrangements for local authority housing investment with the increasing variations in local housing requirements. An effective new system must:

—give authorities the opportunity to frame their proposals for meeting local requirements by public sector investment in the most appropriate way;

—lead to assessments of requirements which are sufficiently uniform to serve as a basis for judging between the claims of different areas.

9.07 The Secretary of State for the Environment announced in November 1976 the Government's intention to introduce a system of 'housing investment programmes'. These will be a new form of housing plan, based on a comprehensive assessment of the local housing situation. The main element will be a reasoned capital budget covering the local authority's own capital spending plans—related to its broad housing strategy—for the coming 4 years. On the basis of these plans, the Government will make capital spending allocations to each authority. Once the allocations are settled, authorities will be free to go ahead with the minimum of intervention by central Government. A similar approach will be developed in Wales.

9.08 The housing investment programme will cover the full range of local authority housing activities—clearance and demolition, renovation, conversion, home loans, improvement grants to private householders, and acquisition, as well as new building—against the background of provision by the private sector and other public sector bodies. To ensure reasonable uniformity in the preparation of programmes, the Department of the Environment will shortly be issuing advice, based on work now in progress by its Housing Services Advisory Group, on methods of assessing housing requirements.

9.09 The transition to this new approach will take place in 1977/78. But the full development of the new system—building up a comprehensive picture of housing requirements area by area and working out the details of operation in consultation with local authority representatives—will take a number of years. There is much to learn.

9.10 The housing investment programme will offer a number of advantages for central Government and for local authorities.

—It will provide a means of controlling public expenditure while allowing resources to be allocated selectively with regard to variations in local housing requirements. Within the context of national policies and standards it will increase local discretion by putting greater responsibility for deciding the right mix of investment on the local authorities. For instance, they will be able to decide for themselves the balance to be struck between acquiring and if necessary renovating existing houses, and building new ones.

—It will give authorities an incentive to seek the most cost-effective mix of spending programmes to meet their requirements.

—It will encourage local authorities to adopt a comprehensive approach to housing provision, including provision for those with special needs.

—It will provide some flexibility to alter spending within a financial year and from one year to another, as circumstances change, thus improving the use of time, resources, and cash when unforeseen opportunities or problems arise.

9.11 The new system of housing investment programmes should also provide an opportunity for introducing greater room for manoeuvre and cost-consciousness into other aspects of the design and control of new housing schemes.

—*New methods of cost control.* The present 'housing cost yardstick' involves too much detailed and time-consuming work for both central and local government. Discussions have suggested that a simpler system, based on a fixed level of costs per house eligible for subsidy combined with monitoring of overall cost trends, could provide local authorities with greater incentives to seek value for money in their building schemes and cut down on paper work. This new approach will be developed in further consultation with the local authorities.

—*Improved accounting procedures.* The statutory 'Housing Revenue Account' (HRA) is not adequate as a tool for effective financial planning. The Government propose to discuss with the local authorities the possibility of introducing new forms of accounts. These could, for instance, enable authorities to identify and monitor separately the costs of land holding, new development, and estate management. The Government also wish to explore the case for re-introducing a statutory repairs account linked to the new arrangements for subsidy, discussed later, as a means of making regular provision for some of the more substantial but intermittent costs of repair and renewal.

These proposals could provide a key to obtaining better value for money for the local authority and the whole community.

TYPES OF HOUSING

9.12 In taking a strategic view of their responsibilities for housing in their area, local authorities will need to consider varieties of provision and demand to an extent which is only beginning to be explored.

9.13 What people would like in the way of a house or flat may depend not only on the size of their household and the ages of those concerned, but also on their likes and dislikes and their particular lifestyles. It is wrong to impose preconceived ideas on people against their wishes. Some people prefer to live in a modernised Edwardian 'two-up, two-down' rather than a newer house. Some young couples may be happy to begin life together in a small 'starter' home rather than wait for a larger but more expensive house. Some single people prefer to live in bedsitters or to share.

9.14 Both housing and planning authorities will need to ensure that widely differing requirements are met. This will call for a flexible approach to residential densities, reflecting local conditions, and the Department of the Environment will be issuing advice on this shortly. It will also require a greater willingness to accept less conventional types, sizes, and forms of accommodation. For example:

—New public sector housing should provide a carefully worked out range of dwelling types and sizes, taking account of needs which are not being met by the private sector. Provision should not be restricted to households whose requirements can be met by a relatively narrow range of housing types.

—The use of older housing requires an imaginative approach to such matters as space standards, room arrangements and the type of households for whom the premises might prove attractive.

—Steps should also be taken to promote and encourage the provision of a range of housing types in the private sector to meet local requirements. Housing and planning authorities should bear in mind that the internal arrangement of dwellings is not a matter for development control; and Parker Morris standards are not applicable to the private sector where authorities have no control over the size of household occupying the dwellings.

—Some people like or need to live in town or city centres. The value of this for the towns and cities themselves has long been recognised.

—The role of mobile homes for small households should be considered. A Review of Mobile Homes is currently in progress.

9.15 The increasing range of housing requirements will make new demands on the public sector and will make it necessary to ensure that housing standards are not drawn up in a way that discourages variety of provision. The Department of the Environment and the Welsh Office are reviewing the scope for introducing greater flexibility into public sector standards, and will be consulting local authority representatives.

LOCAL AUTHORITY ALLOCATION PRACTICES

9.16 If local authorities are to be successful in coping with changes in the pattern of housing need, the new investment system must be matched by changes in the allocation of housing. In areas where there is a shortage of housing, it would be wrong to change allocation policy so as to improve the housing prospects of, for example, a couple without children sharing a physically adequate house with another household at the expense of more traditional categories of housing need, such as a family with children living in overcrowded conditions, or elderly or disabled people who need special help. But as the most serious housing problems are gradually overcome, an increasing number of authorities should be able to spread their net more widely.

9.17 The Government consider that all authorities should be reconsidering their allocation policies, to ensure that they are able to judge the priorities to be given to new categories of applicant alongside those currently given priority. The new categories would include those who have in the past looked to the private rented sector for housing, such as couples without children, single working people and students, and mobile households who cannot count on staying in one place for any length of time.

9.18 The needs of some, though not all, of these people can often be met by using property which is difficult to let to families. As local pressures on housing relax, some authorities are finding that certain types of housing— notably high rise blocks, deck-access blocks and older walk-up blocks—can be suitable for others in need of accommodation. A number of authorities are already allocating property of this sort to people whose claims have not previously been given priority.

9.19 Authorities should also look closely at their policies for allocating municipalised housing. This will often have been acquired from the private rented sector, and may be specially suitable for housing those who are unable to obtain accommodation in that sector. A large house formerly in multiple occupation, for example, may be better kept in that use, to house single people, than converted into self-contained flats.

9.20 But the Government wish to maintain their policy of giving the maximum freedom to authorities to interpret and implement national policies in the light of local circumstances. They therefore believe that proposals to control local authorities' allocation policies centrally—for example by laying down a statutory framework for allocation schemes—should be rejected, with the following two exceptions:

—ending the practice of imposing residential or other qualifications for inclusion on a housing list;

—requiring publication of allocation schemes.

9.21 On the first exception, the Government share the view of the Cullingworth Committee* that it is 'fundamental that no one should be precluded from applying for, or being considered for, a council tenancy on any ground whatsoever'. Today, eight years after the Committee reported, the practice of requiring a period of residence is still widespread. The case for legislation will be considered.

9.22 As regards the second, a local authority's method of allocating housing must be seen to be fair. The Government will introduce legislation requiring allocation schemes to be published. Such a requirement need not entail impersonal or rigid procedures. But the criteria for allocation must be clear.

THE ROLE OF HOUSING ASSOCIATIONS

9.23 Housing association activity has grown dramatically since the Government introduced a new system of financial support in the Housing Act 1974. During the last three years, projects have been approved which will in total provide nearly 100,000 units by new building and over 50,000 units by rehabilitation and conversion, as compared with total provision by housing associations of some 40,000 units in the preceding 3 years. The housing association programme is currently running at an annual level of about 20,000 units by new building, and about 15,000 by rehabilitation and conversion. The provisions of the 1974 Act which restrict Exchequer support to housing associations registered by the Housing Corporation are designed to ensure that this expansion of activity is entrusted only to properly managed and accountable associations.

9.24 Housing associations have a particularly important role to play in contributing variety and flexibility to the public sector. They are sometimes better able than local authorities to provide for households who need to be fairly mobile, such as single people of working age, and for special groups such as the elderly, the disabled, and the one-parent family, who may need special help. Housing associations have also played an increasingly important role in recent years in acquiring and improving run-down older houses, often in inner city areas, and converting them into the sort of smaller unit for which demand frequently exceeds the available supply. Voluntary organisations formed to meet special needs can be helped to achieve their objectives if they are registered as housing associations.

9.25 The Government want to see a continuing growth of the activities of registered housing associations. The development of effective local housing strategies will call for even closer co-operation with local authorities. Housing associations must play their part within the local strategies, while not in any way sacrificing the capacity to meet special needs which is one of their most valuable characteristics. Where local authorities have nomination rights over housing association tenancies, they can use them to introduce more flexibility into their allocation policies and extend the range of households for whom they cater.

*Council Housing: Purposes, Procedures and Priorities. Report of the Central Housing Advisory Committee (HMSO, 1969; paragraph 169.)

9.26   With the growing importance of the housing associations' role, and the larger size of many associations, informal methods of allocation which have been adequate in the past may no longer be appropriate. The Government consider that it should be normal practice for all but the smallest associations to publish the basis on which they allocate tenancies.

THE ROLE OF NEW TOWNS

9.27   The new towns have been internationally acclaimed for their achievement in housing three-quarters of a million people, most of them in houses with gardens, in a good environment, with jobs, schools, shops and other facilities on the doorstep. They have been responsible for pioneering new approaches in planning new communities, in housing design and layout and in landscaping. Altogether the English and Welsh new towns have built some 220,000 houses, and in recent years have been responsible for a tenth of the public sector rented programme.

9.28   Tenancies in new towns have been allocated very largely on the basis of providing houses for workers needed to man new town industries and services. This has led to the criticism that they have housed young skilled workers, leaving behind in the inner cities the old, the unskilled and the socially disadvantaged. It is true that the new towns have largely attracted the sort of industries which employ a high proportion of skilled workers. But the social structure in many of the towns differs very little from the national average. There is more truth in the charge that the new towns have taken only the young. Many of those who have moved have been young married couples. But in more recent years increasing provision has been made, especially in the older new towns, to house the now elderly parents of the original new town families, and the Government would like to see a further move in this direction.

9.29   Recent Government statements have stressed the need to achieve a new balance between development within the cities and development outside. This does not mean that there is no future for the new towns. There are still some inner city areas, as the Lambeth study* shows, which depend on some further dispersal of population if decent living conditions are to be created for those who remain. New towns will also continue to have a role as industrial growth points. In the past they have shown themselves to be capable of responding to changing circumstances, and they will continue to do so. In particular they need to house an increasing proportion of the elderly and disadvantaged people who are willing to move from the inner cities; and they should be prepared to meet the growing demand for home ownership.

LOCAL AUTHORITY SUBSIDIES

9.30   The basic aim of all local authority subsidy systems is to bridge the 'gap' between what it costs a local authority to provide decent housing and the amount which the local community should be asked to pay for such housing, both directly through rents and indirectly by means of contributions to the

---

*Inner Area Studies: Summaries of Consultants' Final Reports (HMSO, 1977).

HRA from the General Rate Fund. To do this effectively in current circumstances, the subsidy system has to be able to take account of three major factors:

—*The need for subsidy varies greatly from one area to another.* Both housing problems themselves, and the resources on which a local authority can draw, differ very widely. The benefits of a system of capital allocation which can recognise different degrees of need will not be realised unless the subsidy system also can respond to the great variety in the circumstances of local authorities;

—*Changes in general financial circumstances, particularly in the level of interest rates, significantly affect the need for subsidy.* Investment in areas with large new building programmes—often with a large backlog of unmet housing need—is in danger of being cut back if there is a sharp increase in capital costs, and more importantly in interest rates, unless the subsidy system can help to take the strain (see Chapter 4). But when interest rates are comparatively stable, a larger proportion of costs can often be met by rents without imposing undue burdens on tenants.

—*Different authorities are affected in different ways by financial changes.* This depends mainly on their need for new investment, and on the age structure of their housing stock (see paragraph 5.25).

The present subsidy system

9.31 The present subsidy arrangements for local authorities were introduced in the Housing Rents and Subsidies Act 1975 which repealed the 'fair rent' basis of rent fixing introduced in the Housing Finance Act of 1972. The 1975 Act restored to local authorities the freedom to fix the rents of their dwellings, and to determine the balance between rent income and General Rate Fund support, subject to the rule that in determining reasonable rent levels local authorities should not budget for a surplus on the HRA, other than a reasonable working balance.

9.32 The 1975 Act subsidy system—designed as an interim arrangement pending the outcome of the Housing Policy Review—has four main elements:

  (i) a 'basic element'—a consolidation and continuation of the subsidy received by each authority in the last year of the 1972 Act's operation;

  (ii) a 'new capital costs element'—a 66 per cent subsidy towards the annual loan charges arising from approved capital works;

  (iii) A 'supplementary financing element'—33 per cent subsidy on any increase in loan charges on the subsidisable debt as at 31 March 1975;

  (iv) a 'special element' (for 1975–77) and a 'high costs element' (paid from 1976/77) for those authorities with exceptionally high costs.

9.33 This system has certain rigid characteristics which would not make it acceptable as a permanent arrangement. For example, the 'basic element', which is fixed in money terms, may be over-generous to authorities with small investment programmes where the burden of debt is declining in relation to tenants' incomes. And the 'new capital costs element', paid as a fixed percentage of loan charges, takes no account either of this factor or of the scope which an authority may have for cross-subsidisation by the 'pooling' of its rents and costs, particularly in periods when interest rates are stable or falling.

Proposed new subsidy system

9.34 The Government consider that a new subsidy system must preserve the rights and duties restored to local authorities by the 1975 Act. To meet the requirements outlined in paragraph 9.30 above, payment of subsidy should be based on a regular appraisal of local housing costs, with the subsidy designed to help bridge the gap, if any, between those costs and a reasonable local contribution from rents and rates. This 'deficit' subsidy should be closely linked with the housing investment programmes for new capital expenditure, while also taking into account necessary current expenditure. The system should work by annual adjustment of subsidy entitlement, to avoid sudden lurches in the amount of assistance provided.

9.35 The details will need to be worked out in consultation with the local authority representatives. But what the Government have in mind is an arrangement on the following lines:

(i) the starting point of the calculation of subsidy would be an authority's entitlement to subsidy in the previous year (starting with the last year of the current system);

(ii) each year a basis for the calculation of *extra* expenditure admissible for subsidy—including extra costs of management and maintenance assessed on an appropriate formula—would be settled for the coming year in consultation with local authorities;

(iii) each year an appropriate level of increase in the 'local contribution' to costs, from rents and rates, would be determined for the coming year, also in consultation with local authorities;

(iv) if the extra admissible expenditure of an authority exceeded the increase in the 'local contribution', subsidy entitlement would be increased. If on the other hand the extra local contribution exceeded this extra expenditure subsidy entitlement would be correspondingly reduced.

9.36 Under this system, the rate of increase in the 'local contribution'—rents and General Rate Fund contribution—would be perhaps the most important decision to be taken annually. It would be the predominant factor in determining the total Exchequer subsidy bill and it would also be likely to influence the size of local authority rent increases, though the balance between rents and General Rate Fund contributions, and the fixing of individual rents, would remain a matter for local discretion.

9.37 It is tempting to argue that the annual rate of rent increases should be determined by reference to some clear principle—for instance, that rents should constitute a fixed proportion of average household income, or that they should meet a minimum proportion of total housing costs. The Government have considered various approaches of this kind, but have found none of them

83

entirely satisfactory. No simple principle can hope to cope with the variations in circumstances which will occur from year to year. One of the advantages of the proposed subsidy system is that it will enable the balance between central and local contributions to housing costs to be struck in the light of all relevant factors, including past and expected movements in incomes, costs and prices. As indicated in Chapters 5 and 6, the Government consider that over a run of years rents should keep broadly in line with changes in money incomes.

9.38 The Government believe that a system on these lines would provide the subsidy necessary to meet essential needs while preserving reasonable economy and efficiency and being fair to tenants, rate-payers and tax-payers alike. It also has the practical advantage of being based on mechanisms with which local authority officers are already familiar. There are of course disadvantages as well as advantages in a system based on annual adjustment. But the Government's view is that, of the various systems suggested in evidence to the Review and considered in the Department of the Environment, this is likely to be the most suitable to meet the diversity of current needs.

9.39 Its effects on individual authorities would vary with their circumstances, and with the decisions taken annually about levels of investment and the local contribution. But in general a system on these lines would tend to ensure that authorities with the biggest 'gap' between their housing costs and their local resources would receive a rather greater proportion of total national subsidy payments than now, while authorities with relatively small investment pro-grammes and correspondingly smaller needs would receive less.

The contribution of local resources

9.40 The larger part of any increase in the local contribution towards costs, and in some cases all of it, should be obtainable from rents without unacceptably large rent increases, especially if the deficit subsidy were payable at a high percentage rate. However, many authorities might still consider it desirable to continue to make a small contribution to their HRA from their General Rate Fund, and high cost authorities might well find it necessary to continue to make a substantial contribution. In addition, all authorities have to make mandatory General Rate Fund contributions to the cost of rent rebates. So the Government expect that General Rate Fund contributions will continue to play a part in the financing of public sector housing.

9.41 At present all General Rate Fund contributions are relevant expenditure for the purposes of calculating rate support grant. The recent Green Paper on the proposals made in the Layfield Report* puts forward for discussion proposals for a new rate support grant system, which would be more closely geared to the expenditure needs of individual authorities. The treatment of Rate Fund contributions to the HRA within this new system, if adopted, would be a matter for further consideration in consultation with the local authorities.

---

*Local Government Finance: Cmnd 6813 (HMSO, 1977).

Coping with irregularities in the pattern of interest payments

9.42 Under the subsidy system outlined here, unexpected increases in costs would be automatically cushioned by additional Exchequer subsidy, which would then be automatically reduced when the need for it had passed. In this way the system would provide a more effective and economical support for investment in the face of fluctuating interest rates than most previous subsidy systems.

9.43 The system would also deal more effectively with the problem of the distorted pattern of real costs over time when interest rates are high and money incomes are rising—the 'front loading' referred to in Chapter 4. Rent pooling already provides a partial solution to this problem. The new subsidy system would go further by giving greater recognition to the high initial costs of interest charges arising from new investment, and by adjusting the amount of subsidy payments from year to year to take account of the fact that the burden of these interest charges tends to decline in relation to incomes when interest rates are steady.

A deferred payment system

9.44 An alternative approach to the problems of 'front loading' considered in the course of the Review would be to provide authorities with additional borrowing facilities to enable them to capitalise part of interest payments on new investment in the early years. This extra borrowing could be added to the original debt and paid back gradually over the originally determined loan period. The effect would be to spread the real burden of repayments more evenly over the repayment period. This approach might offer a useful means of helping individual authorities to cope with the irregularities of interest payments. In the very long term, if virtually the whole of new capital expenditure on housing by local authorities were financed on this basis, the need for general subsidies might be substantially reduced.

9.45 A system which involved such large scale capitalisation of interest would however raise difficult issues of public financing at national and local level, and would be administratively complex. Unless therefore it offered a significant advantage over the proposed new subsidy system in dealing with the problems foreseen over the next decade or so, there would be little point in adopting it. In fact, because there is no satisfactory way of applying the system to existing debt, it could not begin to have a significant effect on HRAs until the 1990s. In the meantime, it would be necessary to supplement it with a separate subsidy system for existing debt.

9.46 The Government consider that, on balance, the possible long-term advantages of a deferred payment system of this kind are not sufficient to justify adopting it in place of—or in conjunction with—the new subsidy system. They do not therefore propose to pursue this.

A minimum subsidy entitlement

9.47 One of the effects of the proposed system over a number of years could be to reduce the subsidy to authorities with a relatively low level of new investment

—indeed, in some cases to phase it out altogether. This raises the question whether general assistance ought to be maintained at some minimum level for all local authorities.

9.48   In Chapter 5, we suggested that it might help to foster a sense of fairness between the owner-occupied and the public rented sectors if some deliberate link were forged between mortgage tax relief and a basic subsidy entitlement. Given the wide differences in the financial arrangements for the two sectors, it is not possible to devise a complete solution to the problem of fairness between them. Nevertheless, it may be thought that a public sector subsidy scheme which gave some local authorities the equivalent of only (say) 10 per cent of their interest charges could not be regarded as even-handed with a structure of tax relief on loans for house purchase which provides all mortgagors with tax relief at a higher percentage rate. These two forms of assistance are not, of course, directly comparable. For example, a local authority normally borrows—and receives subsidy on—the whole of the capital cost of providing housing, whereas the typical mortgagor borrows only 75–80 per cent of the purchase price of a house. A local authority also normally repays housing loans over a period of 60 years; the borrowing costs—and hence the entitlement to subsidy—are larger for such long-term loans than for the much shorter period (say 30 years with successive mortgages) for which most home owners have loans outstanding. But these differences could be taken into account as necessary in determining a relationship between rates of assistance with interest in the two sectors.

9.49   A link could be established by fixing a minimum subsidy entitlement which would set a limit to the process of increase in the 'local contribution' to costs from rents and rates. When this 'subsidy floor' was reached, subsidy would be held steady. Rents would then fall gradually in real terms, as the tenants of the authority as a group enjoyed the full benefits of fixed historic costs in the same way in which home owners individually enjoy the full benefit of a gradually declining real level of costs under conventional mortgage arrangements.

9.50   The Government put forward for public discussion the idea of a 'subsidy floor' related to tax relief at the basic rate as a possible approach to the achievement of a greater sense of fairness as between local authority tenants and home owners.

A national rent pool

9.51   One of the consequences of the proposed new subsidy system would be a continuation of disparities between rent levels in different parts of the country. Just as a home owner who has paid off his mortgage has to cope only with costs of upkeep, so a local authority in an area where the need for new investment was declining might find that its costs were falling to relatively low levels by comparison with the costs of authorities in pressure areas, and rents could also be allowed to fall in real terms.

9.52   It has been suggested in evidence to the Review—notably by the Housing Centre Trust—that a 'national rent pool' would provide a more rational system of rent fixing which would even out these disparities. Just as each individual local authority evens out the burden of costs by setting rents so as to cover costs in aggregate, rather than relating the rents of individual houses to the cost of providing those houses, so, it is argued, a national account should be introduced through which those authorities with relatively low housing costs could contribute to the costs of authorities with greater financial burdens.

9.53 There is an important objection of principle to this proposal. A national rent pool would require some local authorities to produce a surplus on their HRAs, which would be used for the benefit of tenants in different parts of the country. The Government believe that this is unacceptable. If high housing costs in certain areas of the country have to be met by subsidy, it seems right that the cost of the subsidy should fall on the community as a whole, and not solely on local authority tenants in other parts of the country which happen to enjoy relatively low housing costs.

Other subsidy issues

9.54 The new subsidy would be payable to district councils in England and Wales, the London borough councils, the Greater London Council and the Common Council of the City of London. It would not be payable to county councils who are not housing authorities for the purposes of Part V of the Housing Act 1957. In this respect there would be no change from existing arrangements.

9.55 A number of other matters affecting the subsidy arrangements will need to be resolved in consultation with the local authority representatives. They include:

(a) the future treatment of slum clearance subsidy and specific town development subsidies for housing costs;

(b) arrangements for shared equity schemes, housing co-operatives and other new forms of tenure;

(c) the treatment of houses provided to rehouse persons displaced by statutory undertakers;

(d) the treatment of improvement contributions currently payable under the Housing Acts of 1969 and 1971; and

(e) the treatment of houses built expressly for sale.

9.56 It has been suggested that the normal loan repayment period in the public sector—60 years—should be shortened, perhaps to 40 years, in order to reduce the burden of interest payments. Whether in fact there is financial advantage in a shorter loan period depends on what happens over the years to the relationship between inflation and interest rates. But the Government believe that local authorities should have greater freedom to exercise their own judgement about the appropriate repayment period without loss of subsidy entitlement. They therefore propose to make the current rules for borrowing more flexible, whilst retaining the 60-year basis for payment of subsidy.

87

HOUSING SUBSIDIES FOR NEW TOWNS AND HOUSING ASSOCIATIONS

9.57 The Government envisage that the proposed new subsidy system could be applied to New Town Development Corporations and the Development Board for Rural Wales, with appropriate adjustments to take account of the lack of a General Rate Fund.

9.58 There is also a case for applying a subsidy system on these lines to registered housing associations. The housing association grant system introduced by the Housing Act 1974 has been successful in stimulating housing associations' activities but it has serious defects. The calculation of once-for-all capital grants on completion of each project creates a great deal of work for all concerned, implies assumptions about the future course of rent levels and running costs which involve great uncertainty, and does not allow for recovery of excess grant if inflation subsequently reduces the real burden of loan charges to more manageable levels.

9.59 Under the proposed subsidy system, registered housing associations could be treated on very similar lines to local authorities. The difference between the total expenditure reasonably incurred by an association and the total income which it could reasonably be expected to recover from tenants would rank for subsidy. The 'base year' subsidies from which subsequent annual adjustments would be made would comprise all subsidies to which an association was entitled under current legislation, including revenue deficit grant.

9.60 The main question to be resolved in applying the subsidy system to housing associations would be the basis for rent determination. It would be possible to go on using 'fair rent' income as the basis for annual subsidies under the new system. On the other hand, there would be certain advantages—in terms of achieving a more logical relationship with local authority rents—in removing registered housing associations from the fair rent system and making them responsible, under the supervision of the Housing Corporation, for adjusting individual rents on a pooled basis across their estate so as to balance their revenue account. Starting from existing rent levels, average rent increases would be assumed each year analogous to the increase in the local contribution assumed in the local authority subsidy system.

9.61 This and other detailed questions about the implications of the proposed system for housing associations will be considered in early consultations with the Housing Corporation and the National Federation of Housing Associations.

9.62 Special legislative arrangements were made for the North Eastern Housing Association under the Acts of 1972 and 1975. If changes are made on the lines proposed for housing associations generally, it will be for further consideration, in consultation with the Association and local authority representatives, whether they can appropriately be applied to the Association.

CONCLUSIONS

9.63 Much of this chapter has been about the need for local authorities, in conjunction with the other public sector bodies, to develop new approaches to the changing problems of their areas—to carry out more comprehensive assessments of the local housing situation, and to adopt the more flexible allocation practices which will be needed as authorities respond to increasingly varied demands. Authorities have shown before now that they are well able to respond to change. Much of what is said above reflects the adjustments which some authorities are already making in response to a changing situation.

9.64 But it is vitally important that this sort of response is now developed by *all* housing authorities. The powers of central Government in housing matters are inevitably limited. They must set the legislative framework and distribute the resources available for investment. They can provide a subsidy system of the sort described earlier which is consistent with national housing policy and reflects local needs. They can advise and persuade. But the real effectiveness of the public sector's contribution to the solution of our housing problems depends on the way in which national policies are applied 'on the ground'—on the energy and foresight of the members who take the local decisions. Non-one should under-estimate the importance—or the difficulty—of their tasks.

CHAPTER 10

The Housing Stock

10.01 The previous three chapters have looked at each of the main housing sectors separately. But some important issues of housing policy cut across the tenure boundaries. Many of these are inter-related, and cannot be regarded as separate from one another. For the purposes of exposition they are grouped as follows:

—this chapter looks at *improvement policy* and at action by local authorities to secure *fuller use* of the existing stock;

—Chapter 11 looks at *housing tenure;*

—Chapter 12 looks at *problems faced by individuals* in getting suitable housing.

IMPROVEMENT POLICY

10.02 There have been major developments in improvement policy during the last ten years. The most significant has probably been the concept of area improvement. The Housing Act 1969, in addition to overhauling the system of improvement grants*, introduced 'general improvement areas' (GIAs); the aim was to save areas of fundamentally sound older houses, by encouraging residents and owners to bring the houses themselves up to a good standard with the aid of grant, and by improving their surroundings. By the end of March 1977, about 960 GIAs—containing about 284,000 houses—had been declared in England. A recent survey, based on a sample of one-third of declared GIAs, indicated that in the period 1969–1976 about 35 per cent of all dwellings within GIAs which needed improvement at the time of declaration had in fact been improved.

10.03 The Housing Act 1974 brought grant levels up to date, made changes in the standards determining the payment of grant, and revised the rules governing availability of grant. It also reinforced the 1969 Act's 'area' approach by the introduction of Housing Action Areas (HAAs). Unlike GIAs, HAAs are areas of poor housing and of social stress. House improvement may be more difficult to achieve since more houses are likely to be unfit, lacking amenities, or in disrepair, and household resources are likely to be lower. Local authority intervention, through the acquisition of houses or use of compulsory improvement powers, may be necessary to secure improvements during the five year 'life' of the declaration. Up to the end of March 1977 about 190 HAAs—containing about 68,000 houses—had been declared in England. Progress in HAAs has been rather slower than had been hoped, because of the multiplicity of problems which are often found.

10.04 It is too early to judge the effectiveness of the changes made by the 1974 Act—especially the HAA concept—and to make major new proposals. Nevertheless it is right to review the adequacy of current provisions for renovation and maintenance of the housing stock; and to consider whether renovation policies

---

*'Improvement grant' is used in this chapter for all types of grants for improvement work.

are being sensibly and effectively administered, and how far rehabilitation can be used to deal with problems of areas, particularly in the inner cities, which are suffering from overcrowding, neglect and decay.

OBJECTIVES

10.05 Renovation policy has two broad objectives—

(i) a social objective—to enable those who live in poor quality older housing to bring it up to a decent standard as quickly as possible; this often needs to be matched by action to improve the surroundings as well;

(ii) an economic objective—to minimise the waste of resources resulting from the neglect and decay of houses which still have useful life in them if brought up to a decent level of amenity and repair.

10.06 Renovation can bring wider environmental benefits. The gradual improvement of an area of older houses, matched by action to improve their surroundings, can lead to the progressive renewal of a familiar neighbourhood, which most people prefer to large-scale clearance and redevelopment. Now that most of the Victorian slums have been dealt with, it will be possible to adopt this gradual approach in more of our cities. The Government welcome this, and believe that renovation must become an increasingly important element in housing policy over the next decade.

10.07 There will always be some houses which reach the end of their useful life and have to be demolished. The choice between demolition and renovation can only be decided in the light of the condition of the particular houses in question and their surroundings. But the Government believe that the potential benefits of renovation need to be more carefully assessed in future. If older houses can be made decent for a good number of years for less than the cost of redevelopment, this is economically good sense, scarce resources can be stretched further, and the housing conditions of more people can be improved more quickly. If a neighbourhood can be preserved and improved gradually rather than torn down, the sense of community which may cling to a familiar row of shops, a school, or a pub, can be preserved and reinforced. All of these factors must be taken into account in weighing the advantages of renovation against the alternatives.

RECENT PROGRESS

10.08 First results from the 1976 House Condition Survey in England are just becoming available. At the time of the survey there were 794,000 unfit houses compared with an estimated 1,147,000 when the last survey was undertaken in 1971. The reduction of some 350,000 results from an estimated 440,000 houses which were unfit in 1971 being made fit, 350,000 houses becoming unfit in the intervening period and 260,000 unfit houses being demolished. The proportion of unfit houses which are within potential clearance areas has fallen sharply; in 1971 691,000 unfit houses were within potential clearance areas out of the total of 1,147,000 such houses. In 1976 only 347,000 out of 794,000 were so classified.

D

10.09 There has been a similar downward trend in the number of houses which, whilst not unfit, lack one or more of the basic amenities. From a total of 1,748,000 such houses in England in 1971 the number has now fallen to 921,000.

10.10 The distribution of unfit houses and houses lacking amenities between the three main tenure groups in 1971 and 1976 was as follows:

TABLE 4
UNFIT HOUSES AND HOUSES LACKING BASIC AMENITIES, 1971 AND 1976 (ENGLAND)

		England: thousands			
		Owner-occupied	Rented from LA/NT	Private rented etc.	Vacant or closed	All tenures
Unfit	1971	318	58	606	165	1,147
	1976	263	46	334	151	794
Fit but lacking one or more basic amenities...	1971	619	445	601	83	1,748
	1976	278	255	343	45	921

10.11 Whilst these figures demonstrate a welcome reduction in the amount of unsatisfactory housing, the rate of progress does not match the very sharp rise in grant-aided improvement expenditure—from about £146m in 1970/71 to £749m in 1973/74, though with a subsequent decline to £490m in 1975/76 (England—1976/77 prices).

10.12 Exactly parallel figures for Wales are not available because of different survey dates. Earlier surveys suggested a substantial *increase* in the number of unfit houses in Wales between 1968 and 1973. But the first results of the 1976 Welsh House Condition Survey indicate that this trend has been reversed: the number of unfit houses is estimated to have fallen from 147,000 in 1973 to 100,000 in 1976. As in England, the proportion of these houses in potential clearance areas has also fallen—from 53,000 (36 per cent) to 22,000 (22 per cent). Progress in dealing with substandard housing has been similar to that achieved in England: the number of fit houses without basic amenities has been reduced from 99,000 in 1973 to 63,000 in 1976.

10.13 The results of both surveys are still being analysed. The figures so far available suggest that significant progress has been made in clearing most of the major concentrations of slum houses—but also that in future years not just the extent but the nature of the problem of unfit housing is likely to change. As we deal with the remaining concentrations of slum housing, policies to deal with houses which are already unfit, and with those becoming unfit, will have to be more selective than in the past. The general shift in emphasis away from whole-sale clearance inevitably means that progress in simple numerical terms is likely to be less rapid.

10.14 In the period 1971–1975 over 550,000 improvement grants were given to home owners in England, but despite this there has been a relatively small decrease in the number of unfit houses in this sector. This suggests that the present system of financial support is not achieving the right results. There may well be an increasing problem as the remaining stock of unfit houses in the sector becomes concentrated in the ownership of people who simply cannot afford to take the necessary remedial action, even with the help of grants.

10.15 This problem also applies in the private rented sector where the proportion of unsatisfactory housing remains particularly high. The substantial reduction in the numbers of unfit and sub-standard houses in this sector owes a good deal to changes in tenure—purchase by home owners and local authorities —and to demolition. But some 115,000 houses subject to controlled tenancies were brought up to basic standard (i.e., with all the basic amenities) mainly in the earlier part of the period. The escalating cost of repair and improvement work in the last few years may have affected the rate of improvement of the remaining controlled houses.

10.16 Between 1971 and 1976 there has also been a marked change in the pattern of grants approved for all private owners. In 1971 some 53,000 grants for the installation of basis amenities were given to private owners in England, representing about 45 per cent of all grants given in that sector. The rest were grants paid for work to a higher standard of improvement and repair. By 1975 there were only about 11,000 grants for basic amenities representing some 14 per cent of the total.

10.17 A further significant factor has been the increasing share of expenditure going into public sector improvements. In 1971 less than 20 per cent of occupied houses lacking one or more of the basic amenities were owned by local authorities. In 1969 improvements to local authority houses accounted for about 30 per cent of the total grant-aided improvement work in the public and private sectors. By 1975 that figure had risen to 40 per cent. In 1969 the average cost per house of grant-aided work on local authority housing was about 26 per cent higher than the cost of private sector grant-aided work per house; in 1975 that had risen to a figure 56 per cent higher. Throughout the period 1971–1975 the number of local authority houses improved with the aid of grant was about one-third of the total number of grant-aided improvements in the local authority and private sectors combined. Thus one-third of the improved houses and up to 40 per cent of the grant-aided work were in the sector which at the outset had only one-fifth of the unsatisfactory stock and by 1976 less than one-sixth.

10.18 The 1976 survey also shows a significant increase in the number of houses requiring major repairs. At the time of the previous survey in 1971 it was estimated that some 636,000 houses—including houses unfit and lacking amenities—required expenditure on repairs exceeding £1,000 (at 1971 prices); the latest survey suggests that in 1976 half as many again would need an equivalent amount of expenditure at today's prices (roughly £2,300). Moreover, the 1976 survey also shows that about 1·1 million houses that are neither unfit nor lacking amenities need work costing over £1,000 at today's prices to bring them up to a satisfactory state of repair. The great majority of houses in severe disrepair are in private ownership, divided almost evenly between owner-occupation and rented housing. Action to prevent houses becoming unfit as a result of being allowed to fall into disrepair is likely to be an important aspect of housing policy in the coming years. Without effective measures we shall see the growth of a new generation of slums.

A NEW EMPHASIS

10.19   All this suggests that the tendency over the last few years has been for a growing proportion of the resources devoted to renovation to go into relatively high quality improvements in both sectors, rather than into an attack on the most serious problems—the large numbers of houses, mainly in the private sector, which are either unfit or without basic amenities. The Government believe that a change of emphasis is now called for. For both social and economic reasons, the primary aim must be to rescue as many of these sub-standard houses as possible—to bring them up to a decent standard of amenity and a sound state of repair. If this is not tackled with energy many houses that could be saved will fall into irretrievable decay and many families will have to live in deplorable conditions for years to come.

10.20   The aim should be to deal with the worst improvable houses first. This is not a call for money to be wasted on houses fit only for demolition. Nor is it a call for a policy of 'patching'. But we need to catch more of those houses which, with repair and installation of basic amenities, will provide decent homes for 10 or 20 years to come—and without it will be lost. The Government believe that it is more important to improve a large number of these houses to an adequate basic standard than to improve a smaller number of houses to a higher standard.

10.21   The changes in the grant structure discussed in the following paragraphs should encourage more people to undertake basic improvements and repairs. Over the next few years the effects of the 1974 Housing Act will be systematically monitored and the Government will be developing further their policies on rehabilitation and repair.

GRANTS IN THE PRIVATE SECTOR

10.22   *More flexible administration.* There is some evidence that local authorities are encouraging, in some cases requiring, improvements to a high standard as a condition of grant. Some are reluctant to use the discretionary powers available to them to waive the statutory conditions for payment of grant. The Government will act to encourage a less rigid approach. One possibility under consideration is to provide for payment of grant at a higher rate where houses need to be brought up to a basic standard.

10.23   Since all private sector improvement requires a contribution from the private owner, his confidence in the future of his property must not be under-mined. The 1974 Act requires as a condition of grant that houses shall have a useful life of at least 15 years in the case of grant for the installation of basic amenities, and at least 30 years in the case of the grants paid for improvements to a higher standard. This can be varied within limits at the discretion of the local authority. It is important that they apply these broad yardsticks flexibly. Otherwise they can introduce an undesirable rigidity into the approach to individual improvement applications, and destroy the confidence of a private owner, who may read into the local authority's decision unintended implications in relation to future redevelopment of the area. When this happens it can lead to the progressive and damaging withdrawal of private investment from a whole inner city neighbourhood.

10.24 *Extension of repairs grants.* Under present rules, assistance towards the cost of repairs in most areas is available only if the repairs form part of a scheme of improvement qualifying for grant. If a house has all the basic amenities but is falling into unfitness as a result of structural decay, no grant aid is available unless improvements are carried out at the same time as any necessary repairs.

10.25 This may be a particular problem for elderly home owners who have perhaps spent most of their lives in the house they occupy, and find themselves without the capital to undertake major structural repairs. Some landlords of older properties face similar problems. It is just as important to ensure adequate repair as to promote necessary improvements. The Government therefore propose to make 'repairs only' grants which currently apply only in GIAs and HAAs more widely available, subject to the existing condition that the full cost could not be met by the owner himself without hardship. This has been urged in many of the responses to the reports of the Inner Area Studies published in January 1977, and to the Review of the Rent Acts consultation paper.

10.26 *Cost and Rateable Value Limits.* The major conditions affecting payment of grant are the expense and rateable value limitations on eligibility for grant. The limits on expenses eligible for grant contained an element for anticipated inflation when they were set. But some increase may now be justified, if only in some areas, and this is under consideration. It has been suggested that the rateable value limitations which apply both to improvements (£300 in London, £175 elsewhere) and to conversions (£600 in London, £350 elsewhere) exclude some properties whose improvement or conversion is desirable. The objective of the limits is to exclude from grant owner-occupied dwellings whose improvement can reasonably be met by the owner without special assistance. Rateable values have not generally changed since the limits were originally set, and there is no self-evident case for a general increase in the limits. But the Government will be examining the results of the latest House Condition Survey to see whether there are indications that the present limits are preventing essential renovation work. The Government will consider whether present limits should be changed, either generally or selectively.

10.27 *The private rented sector.* A far higher proportion of the houses in the private rented sector is unfit or substandard than in the other main sectors. The present system of financial assistance for the improvement of properties in this sector is not securing the necessary improvement and there is a real risk that many more houses will decay into unfitness. Some of the reasons for this have to do with matters other than improvement policy, such as the effect of rent controls on the return on capital expenditure. They will be considered in the Review of the Rent Acts. Wider availability of repair grants will help; but there are aspects of improvement policy which may themselves inhibit necessary action.

10.28   The right to apply for any improvement grant is at present conditional upon either ownership of the property to be improved or the holding of a leasehold interest with at least 5 years to run. This means that many tenants in the private rented sector cannot apply for grant towards the cost of improvements even though they are quite willing to invest their own money in improving their home. There is a good case for extending the present conditions on eligibility, to permit tenants to carry out improvements which would not otherwise be done—with no increase in rent resulting from the improvement to the property. This would give many people the opportunity to take steps themselves to improve their own living conditions. This possibility will also be examined within the Review of the Rent Acts.

10.29   Grants ('special grants') are available for the installation of basic amenities in multi-occupied houses at the discretion of the local authority, but there is no allowance for the inclusion of repairs in an improvement scheme. Eligible expense limits are determined by the number of amenities provided.

10.30   Many multi-occupied houses undoubtedly meet a real need, particularly for single-person households or other small households. The Government believe that assistance with the cost of repairs to such houses should be provided. This will be done either by including them within the scope of repair grants, or through the addition of a repairs component within eligible expense limits for special grants.

10.31   There is also a good case for making special grants mandatory rather than discretionary, but it would be necessary to ensure that local authorities retain the power to refuse a grant where a house is clearly unsuitable for multiple occupation.

10.32   *Compulsory improvements.* Local authorities have powers to compel improvement and repair of unsatisfactory housing, but the procedures involved are complex and cumbersome. They will be examined with a view to making them simpler and more effective.

10.33   *Helping the first-time purchaser.* Chapter 7 put forward proposals which will make it easier for first-time buyers to buy cheaper older houses, many of which need improvement and repair. Difficulties have sometimes arisen where both a mortgage and an improvement grant are needed.

—The potential buyer of a house which needs improvement has been in a 'chicken and egg' situation. He could not obtain a loan in many cases until improvements had been made, but the local authority would not make a grant until he owned the property. The Building Societies Association has now advised its members that they might reasonably make a loan if the local authority will indicate informally its intention of making a grant; and local authorities have been encouraged to give such an undertaking in appropriate cases.

—Improvement grants are made on condition that the house retains its present use for at least five years. If this condition is breached, the authority may require repayment with compound interest. But building societies have been concerned that, in a case where the grant has to be repaid, there may be insufficient money left to cover the outstanding debt. Local authorities have now been advised that, although individual cases must be decided on the facts, they are not normally expected to require repayment of a grant when a home owner needs to sell his property, and there is no reason to suppose that the original application for the grant was by an owner who intended to sell at an enhanced value on completion of the improvement work.

Legislation is also proposed to remove the present provision that grants cannot be paid to owner-occupiers of houses in GIAs and HAAs if the house had been let within the previous 12 months.

10.34 *Tax relief and VAT rating on improvement work.* Availability of grants is limited to certain specific types of improvement work. Tax relief is also available on interest paid on loans for 'improvements', though not on loans for 'repairs'; but it may not be generally understood that works such as

—recovering or reconstructing a roof;

—underpinning a house;

—rebuilding a facade;

—insertion or renewal of a damp proof course;

—renewal of electrical installation;

may qualify wholly or partly as improvements for this purpose. For VAT purposes the rules are different and it is immaterial whether a building is improved. Broadly speaking, the zero rate applies to work of alteration, but any work of repair and maintenance is chargeable at the 8 per cent rate. Whether or not a particular job will qualify as an improvement for tax relief or be eligible for VAT zero-rating will depend on just what the job involves. When planning work of this kind it is worth seeking advice on eligibility of loan interest for tax relief (from the Tax Office) and on liability to VAT (from the builder who will be doing the work.)

LOCAL AUTHORITY REHABILITATION

10.35 The new emphasis proposed above—that resources should be concentrated on bringing more older houses up to basic standards—applies to local authorities as well as the private sector. It might for instance mean in some areas that schemes for further improvement of purpose-built local authority houses which already possess all basic amenities should be postponed in favour of essential improvements to houses acquired from the private sector. The need for greater attention to be paid to keeping the housing stock in good repair is also just as important in the public as the private sector. The new subsidy and accounting arrangements proposed in Chapter 9 will help to achieve this.

RENEWAL OPTIONS

10.36 For many older areas the right form of renewal will be a mixture of renovation and redevelopment. The balance will be a decision for the local authority. The existing advice on methods of evaluation is based on a simple calculation about whether improvement would give better value relative to cost than new building. It does not cover the possibility of an effective cost benefit analysis. Further economic advice has therefore been prepared which measures costs and benefits over time and, through discounting techniques, reduces each to a present value. The intention is that the technique should be applied to a range of different courses of action. Each possibility will have different implications for manpower, finance and other resources, and the method of analysis will be designed to assess these on a common basis and select an order of preference in economic terms.

10.37 This technique extends beyond consideration of resource costs incurred by the local authority itself and includes all resources involved in a particular option. There will often be important social costs and benefits which are not readily quantifiable in money terms. These factors will need to be weighed against the net present value derived from the analysis before a final decision is taken. Where the economic costs of redevelopment and rehabilitation are evenly balanced there will normally be a strong case in favour of rehabilitation because of the social benefits. These are not easy decisions to take; and a great deal hangs on making the right choice.

BETTER USE OF THE HOUSING STOCK

10.38 *Empty houses.* As was noted in Chapter 3, a substantial number of houses are bound to be empty at any one time for a variety of reasons: they may be changing hands, undergoing improvement, or awaiting demolition. Some houses stand vacant for long periods for no clear reason. We need to know more about why their owners allow them to remain empty.

10.39 The Government have announced their intention to undertake a sample survey of vacant houses in the autumn of 1977, to get an up-to-date picture of the situation. The survey will examine the causes of vacancy and the length of time houses remain empty, as well as the type and former tenure of the houses and their condition. Its findings will provide information on which to base future action on empty houses. There is no doubt that poor physical condition is one major reason why houses stand empty. The measures described earlier in this chapter for giving a new impetus to the improvement and repair of older houses should themselves bring some empty houses back into use.

10.40 Local authorities have a particular responsibility to ensure that their housing management policies are directed at minimising vacancy rates, and to use their powers and their influence to increase utilisation in the private sector. The acquisition by authorities of vacant houses in areas of housing stress must remain a priority, particularly where property can be brought into use quickly and cheaply. Compulsory purchase powers are available, where necessary, and Government procedures for dealing with compulsory purchase orders on empty houses are to be speeded up. Arrangements already exist for houses owned by Government departments and other public sector bodies to be offered on lease to local authorities when they become temporarily vacant, or for sale when they are permanently surplus to requirements. The Government would also like to see the practice of the leasing of empty privately-owned houses by local authorities being considered more widely. In managing their own stock, local authorities should consider what they can do to reduce vacancy periods to a minimum, for instance by careful programming of improvement work and by more efficient allocation policies.

10.41 *'Under-use'* *of housing* is not easily defined. Different people have different ideas about how much housing space they need or want, and the reasons for under-use vary. Elderly home owners living in family-sized houses may be put off by the cost and inconvenience of moving. In the local authority sector there is sometimes a shortage of smaller accommodation. In the private rented sector, landlords may prefer to leave part of a large house vacant, hoping eventually to regain possession of the whole house.

10.42 A good deal of under-use arises because most of the stock is made up of family-sized houses, and more and more households are small (one and two person). It is no part of the Government's policy to bring unreasonable pressure on people to move to smaller accommodation, or to let rooms. But there is some under-use which arises involuntarily and could be avoided. Many more people might be willing to move, or let spare accommodation, if the obstacles in their way were reduced. There are several ways in which local authorities can help. These include:

—sub-dividing larger houses into smaller units where this is possible;

—making adequate provision in local authority housing investment programmes for smaller houses;

—using 'movement incentives' to enable potential movers to meet transaction costs. Local authorities have a discretionary power (section 93 of the Housing Finance Act 1972) to reimburse removal expenses and other costs, including legal fees, of local authority tenants. Many already make good use of these powers, and others should do so when suitable smaller homes are available.

10.43 The Government are sure that there is scope for making better use of the housing stock, and consider that a variety of measures to improve utilisation should be considered in each area. They will be issuing fuller guidance in a circular to local authorities.

THE LONGER TERM

10.44 The picture emerging from the 1976 House Condition Survey is one of a continued reduction in the amount of unfit and substandard housing but an increasing incidence of major disrepair. We are no longer faced with massive areas of unfit housing, though some substantial clearance programmes remain. But if we are to prevent the emergence of a new generation of slum areas housing policy will have to place growing emphasis on the repair, maintenance and effective use of the existing stock.

Chapter 11

Housing Tenure

11.01 The previous four chapters have been chiefly—though not entirely—concerned with the *provision* and *condition* of housing in each of the three main tenures. But the form of tenure in itself is a matter of great importance to the individual and society. It is one of the Government's main housing objectives that it should become easier for people to obtain the tenure they want; and that as conditions improve, families should be able to look forward to widening opportunities for themselves and their children (see paragraph 2.16 (vii)).

11.02. The measures described in Chapter 7, both on more helpful forms of mortgage facilities—especially the Government's proposed savings bonus and loans schemes—and on the supply of mortgage funds, should bring home ownership into the reach of more people more quickly. The public rented sector already caters for a wide cross section of the population, and the range of household provided for will grow as serious housing problems are overcome. (Chapter 9).

11.03 The expansion of home ownership and the public rented sector means that many people in both these tenures have similar incomes and occupations. The continued growth of those sectors within the framework of the national housing policy will accelerate this trend. The Government welcome this. But they consider that the breaking down of 'compartmentalisation' by tenure should go further by

—the establishment of a tenants' charter designed to ease unnecessary restrictions on tenants;

—the development of new 'intermediate' forms of housing tenure;

—building for sale by the public sector;

—a sensibly regulated programme of sale of public sector rented houses.

11.04 Action on the last three areas of policy will not result in rapid and major national changes in the tenure balance. But the availability of different forms of tenure can contribute powerfully to the regeneration of particular neighbourhoods in a way that cannot be measured in terms of national totals. The development of intermediate forms of tenure in particular can produce an important element of choice and flexibility at the 'margins' of the main tenures, where many acute problems of access can arise. The history of the housing association movement showed that significant results can emerge relatively quickly from new initiatives where there is the will—in 1967 there were only 110,000 housing association houses; in 1976 there were 250,000 (England and Wales).

A TENANTS' CHARTER

11.05 The growth in demand for home ownership and new forms of tenure arises in part from an increasing desire for independence in housing. People welcome the opportunity to be responsible for their own home. A tenant cannot expect quite the same degree of freedom as an owner; but this does not mean that his rights should be unreasonably circumscribed.

Public sector tenants

11.06 Some local authorities impose on their tenants complex rules and regulations, which lay down obligations—often on comparatively detailed matters —but give few rights in return. The Government therefore propose to introduce a Tenants' Charter, developing a code of principles and practices for local authority and new town tenancies, much of which will also be relevant to housing associations.

11.07 *Security of tenure and right to a written agreement.* At present the lack of statutory security of tenure is the most important respect in which the public sector tenant's position falls short of that of tenants in the private sector. Local authority and new town tenants already enjoy a high degree of security in practice, and the Government propose to introduce legislation giving statutory recognition to this 'de facto' security. The special position and responsibilities of housing authorities will be recognised in drawing up the statutory grounds on which possession can be obtained. The Government also believe that public sector tenants should have the statutory right to a written tenancy agreement.

11.08 *A model tenancy agreement.* A tenant should be clear about his rights and obligations. The exact form of these can vary: for example, the rights and obligations of tenants in a high rise block of flats obviously must be different from those of tenants of semi-detached houses. Tenancy agreements should not be unnecessarily restrictive. They should recognise that tenants are responsible, orderly people. All authorities should ensure that tenancy agreements are as simply worded as their status as legal documents permits, and that they are normally accompanied by an explanatory handbook. The Department of the Environment will be issuing guidance after considering, in consultation with the local authority representatives and others, the recommendations in the recently issued report of the Housing Services Advisory Group.*

11.09 The Government consider that tenants should also be given the right to carry out improvements to their homes and to be reimbursed for any substantial improvements they have undertaken when they give up their tenancy. The benefits for the tenants themselves and for better maintenance appear substantial enough to outweigh any management drawbacks. While the landlord's permission should still be required before alterations are made to structure or services, tenancy agreements should make it clear that permission will not be withheld for any reasonable proposals, and that improvements are actively encouraged.

11.10 Those tenants who wish to sub-let rooms in their homes should not be prevented from doing so, or discouraged by the charges added to their rents. Sub-letting can be a valuable way of making better use of the housing stock in areas where accommodation is still short, and can play a useful part in solving problems of mobility for people wishing to take up a job in a new area.

*Tenancy agreements; report by the Housing Services Advisory Group (Department of the Environment, May 1977).

11.11 *Better management.* There is a growing recognition of the importance to tenants of good housing management, but also a widespread feeling that they are not getting it, and that many local authority estates are shabby and poorly maintained. As a generalisation this is probably wide of the mark. But the growth of criticism, and the emergence of problems such as vandalism and difficult-to-let estates, are indications that all is not well. Such problems are often symptomatic of a wider malaise, but the quality of management is certainly an important factor. To some extent the difficulty stems from the pressures on management resources, which have led to economies which may prove to be shortsighted—for example the withdrawal of resident caretakers, who are now being reinstated by some authorities.

11.12 In present economic circumstances improvements in the standard of management must come mainly from skill and efficiency in the use of existing resources rather than spending more. To help achieve this, the Department of the Environment is improving its capacity to give professional advice through the Housing Services Adviser. And consideration is being given to the possibility of a more selective treatment of management and maintenance expenditure in the new subsidy system, to take account of the needs of authorities with problem estates.

11.13 Some management problems may stem from a failure to give tenants a sense of involvement, and of having a stake in their estates. If tenants can have a greater say in running an estate, this will often make them more aware of the problems, and at the same time make management more responsive to their needs. Many local authorities have introduced arrangements for consultation, and for enabling tenants to participate in management decisions. A few are considering giving some of their tenants a formal, contractual, status. Tenants can also be given access to or be co-opted to local authority committees or advisory panels. At estate level, they can assist in framing rules and regulations, and possibly in allocation. They might also be given freedom to decide how to spend an assigned budget on cleaning, garden maintenance, minor improvements, community activities, etc. But this is not an area in which a uniform practice can be imposed. The Department of the Environment are sponsoring a handbook containing advice to local authorities on how to set up and run schemes for tenant participation, and are preparing 'Neighbourhood Action Packs' designed to aid and encourage tenants who wish to participate.

11.14 *Housing Co-operatives.* These arrangements can be taken a stage further by the formation of housing co-operatives. In the Housing Rents and Subsidies Act 1975 the Government introduced arrangements whereby local authorities can enter into contractual arrangements not only to transfer management functions to tenant co-operatives but to lease property to them, without loss of subsidy. The Final Report of the Working Party on Housing Co-operatives was published in January 1976. Subsequently strong Government support was given to development of housing co-operatives in DOE Circular 8/76 and Welsh Office Circular 15/76. The first experimental projects in this field are now being undertaken—for example by the London Borough of Haringey.

11.15 Not all tenants will wish to assume full control of their estates; but the Government believe that all local authorities should take steps to explain to their tenants what housing co-operatives involve, and to find out whether they would be willing to take part in such schemes.

11.16 Housing associations, with their smaller scale of operations, can play an important part in setting up co-operatives, both by the transfer of management responsibilities to tenants of existing estates and by helping private sector tenants to take over the control and ownership of their homes on a co-operative basis. The success of tenant co-operatives in areas of serious housing stress in North London and Liverpool has demonstrated that co-operatives do not discriminate—as some have suggested—against those in housing need. The Housing Corporation, at the Government's request, has set up the Co-operative Housing Agency to provide guidance and financial support.

11.17 The Government have also announced their intention of amending existing legislation to make it easier to set up housing co-operatives. This would include widening the powers of the Housing Corporation to bring the promotion of housing co-operatives firmly within their remit; dealing with problems of stamp duty; and reviewing the eligibility for rent allowances of members of co-operatives.

Private tenants

11.18 Tenants in the private rented sector already have a legal right to security of tenure. But there may be ways analogous to those proposed for public sector tenants of improving their position. As a first step consideration is being given in the Review of the Rent Acts to offering private tenants the right to carry out improvements and repairs and to apply for the appropriate grants in certain circumstances where the landlord is unwilling to carry out the work himself (see paragraph 10.28).

11.19 The possible scope for giving private tenants the right to come together and purchase their homes, where blocks are up for sale and where it can be done within a co-operative framework, will be considered.

'INTERMEDIATE' TENURES

11.20 The Government are encouraging local authorities and housing associations to explore arrangements designed to provide some of the advantages of ownership and tenancy, both as a stepping stone to full home ownership, and as a permanent form of tenure. Such arrangements offer greater control over living conditions and an opportunity to share in capital appreciation.

11.21 The 'non-equity' co-operatives, referred to in paragraphs 11.14–11.17, provide tenants collectively with many of the advantages of ownership, but they do not allow them to participate individually in financial benefits arising from the growth in the value of the property. Co-ownership schemes combine co-operative management with individual equity sharing. The housing is provided by a co-operative association of which all the tenants are members.

Rent payments cover management and maintenance costs and service the joint mortgage. Option mortgage subsidy is available, and tenants are entitled, when they leave the scheme, to a payment based upon the increase in the value of the property as reflected in the rent at which it can be re-let. Hitherto co-ownership schemes have received no assistance other than option mortgage subsidy, and so new schemes have tended to be severely affected by high costs and interest rates.

11.22 In order to revive co-ownership housing the Housing Corporation have been asked to implement a pilot programme of schemes in which housing association grant is paid on part of the capital cost. This reduces the unsubsidised cost, and therefore the rent to be paid, but the financial stake of members in the equity is proportionately reduced.

11.23 This Housing Corporation pilot programme also includes equity sharing schemes involving individual leaseholds. The occupier buys half the equity, and pays rent on the other half, which remains in the ownership of a housing association and is eligible for housing association grant. Under present legislation this scheme cannot lead to full ownership but the Government intend to remove this constraint in order to permit housing associations to build for sale, either outright or on an equity-sharing basis.

11.24 The pilot programme also includes schemes for the elderly to buy part of the equity in a new home with the proceeds of selling the old family house. Here again the remaining part of the equity stays in public ownership and is eligible for grant.

11.25 Local authorities have also been involved in equity-sharing schemes. The pioneering venture in this field was the 'half-and-half' mortgage scheme introduced by Birmingham City Council. Under the scheme, the occupier acquires a long lease on his house (with a local authority mortgage) for a premium equal to half the cost, and also pays half the rent he would pay as a local authority tenant. The occupier is responsible for repairs and maintenance, but is largely free from the standard tenancy conditions and may make improvements or alterations to the house subject to the terms of the lease. He may also at any time purchase the freehold for half the current value of the house. But for the first five years after the grant of the lease the City Council have first option to buy back the lessee's share at the price he paid, if he wishes to dispose of it.

11.26 Several other authorities are interested in promoting schemes of this type for newly-built houses and a few have already done so. This is still new territory, but with a bit more experience we should learn the answers to some of the questions which have been raised. For instance:

—Should it be possible to vary the proportions of the capital cost covered by the lease and the rent respectively, and if so, what adjustments need to be made—for example, should the occupier still be responsible for maintenance costs, even if the leased share represents much less than half of the capital cost?

104

—How satisfactory is equity sharing as a permanent arrangement?

—What considerations are involved in applying equity sharing schemes to the existing public rented sector stock? There certainly seems to be scope for applying the 'half-and-half' principle to newly municipalised property so as to recycle the funds for acquisition and improvement of older housing.

11.27 The building societies have an important part to play in providing mortgage finance for equity sharing schemes, as they have in the past for traditional home ownership, and the Government hope that it will be possible to devise arrangements which enable them to support such schemes.

11.28 The various arrangements described above are only a few drawn from a wide spectrum of possible forms of 'intermediate' tenure. The Government want to encourage further new ventures. Other possibilities include:

—arrangements under which property purchased by private sector tenants from their landlords is held on a mixture of tenures (eg individual long leases and ordinary renting) within a co-operative management framework;

—equity sharing arrangements between private landlords and their tenants.

BUILDING FOR SALE

11.29 For many years local authorities have built new houses for sale or for letting on a long lease. The scale of activity has been comparatively small, since authorities have not sought to compete in the housebuilding market but have provided houses for sale—either directly or through local authority sponsored schemes undertaken by developers—for those who might otherwise have looked to them for a house to rent. Building for sale has usually implied the construction of new houses, but authorities are now exploring the scope for conversion or rehabilitation of houses or flats for sale or lease.

11.30 Building for sale has several merits. It offers many people a home of their own at a reasonable price. It can enable them to stay in their own community instead of seeking a cheaper house elsewhere. And it can relieve pressure as existing tenants or applicants from the waiting list are enabled to buy their own homes. Local authorities will continue to meet the great majority of the housing needs that they have to satisfy by providing houses to rent; but in allocating the resources available to them they should take account of the opportunities to meet need by building for sale.

11.31 Hitherto, building for sale by local authorities has been seen as a useful way of providing for the cheaper end of the home ownership market and for small households including people who live on their own. Its impact has been substantial in the localities where schemes have been undertaken; and its contribution to inner city neighbourhoods could be of great significance. Authorities should not concentrate solely on meeting immediate housing demands but should also consider the housing needs of workers in incoming industry and commerce so that they attract newcomers as well as retaining the existing population. Where private developers are not meeting this demand local authorities may feel justified in building houses for sale over a wider spectrum of the home ownership market than might be appropriate in other areas.

11.32 The Government would welcome on extension of building for sale. The Department of the Environment are issuing a paper describing a number of existing schemes in various parts of the country as an illustration of what has been and can be achieved. It will contain general information to help interested local authorities and developers.

11.33 Although the discussion in this section has been in terms of building for outright sale, the procedures involved are essentially the same if local authorities are promoting building for the newer forms of tenure—for example half and half schemes—discussed in the preceding section. In both cases it will be important for local authorities to co-operate with housebuilders and building societies, especially so as to encourage the production of reasonably priced housing outside the traditional rented sector in inner city areas.

SALE OF COUNCIL HOUSES

11.34 The Government recognise that some families whose lives and affections are rooted in a particular house in a familiar neighbourhood wish to buy their home. But the consideration of whether in the particular circumstances of an area the authority should sell some of its houses raises wide and sensitive issues.

11.35 In favour of selling council houses it is argued that the wishes of the existing tenant will be met and support given to an underlying trend to home ownership. Indeed it has been suggested that the wishes of the council tenant should be paramount and that he should be given a statutory right to buy. Sales may benefit the community since they may keep families within an area from which they might otherwise have moved and also since they may lead to a desirable mix of tenures. The standard of maintenance may be improved since the home owner will normally put in extra effort and resources to keeping his house in good shape. Finally, it is argued that there are considerable financial advantages in that sales relieve central Government from paying subsidy and the local authority from borrowing and making rate fund contributions; and that where sales are financed from private sector sources they make more money available which could go into additional housing provision.

11.36 On the other hand major disadvantages are seen in sales. There is concern about the damage done to an authority's ability to meet housing need, particularly in areas where there is a shortage of rented accommodation, through the loss of relets (the loss of relets is in the order of 3 per cent to 5 per cent a year). There is also a fear that the most desirable stock will be sold, that is houses with gardens, leaving the authority with the properties that are more difficult to let. And it is argued that the financial advantages are ephemeral since, over time, the Government will pay out more in mortgage tax relief than in subsidies and that the local authority's Housing Revenue Account will suffer since rents will increase against interest charges held to a historically determined debt and thereby reverse a short-term financial advantage.

11.37   On this last point, definitive comment is difficult because to some extent the advantages will depend on local circumstances. In the short term, so far as it is possible to make a general assessment, it appears that for most housing the revenue from sales will exceed the rent and Government subsidy which was previously received, less the cost of management and maintenance. Over the longer term the position changes. But calculations of this sort, stretching over a long period, depend very much on what assumptions are made about inflation, interest rates, costs and rents. For the other arguments, the answer must lie mainly in a careful judgement made in the light of local circumstances. Authorities' policies coupled with demand to buy council houses in their areas have led to a comparatively modest level of sales. In England and Wales as a whole, just over 130,000 council dwellings have been sold during the past 10 years. (Sales reached a peak of 45,000 in 1972 but for the last three years, during which the general consent to sell has remained available, sales have run at an average of less than 5,000 a year.) In contrast, during the same 10 year period authorities have completed some 1·1 million houses; and their total stock is now estimated at about 5·3 million.

11.38   The Government have followed a clear policy. They do not favour sales where this would reduce the provision of rented accommodation where there is an unmet demand. That is why the Government reject a statutory right for tenants to buy. Indeed, it would be anomolous for the Government to direct their policies and priorities, as they have done, to the assistance of areas of housing stress and at the same time to accept a substantial depletion of the kind of stock which they are encouraging authorities to provide. But the Government see no reason to object where the improving local circumstances are such that sales on reasonable terms would not impair an authority's ability to offer accommodation to rent to those in housing need or the quality of their stock.

11.39   The Government adhere to that general policy. They consider that an authority's proposals to sell should be seen as part of the total approach to housing for the area, including in particular its proposals for meeting needs for rented accommodation of the right type and quality. For most authorities, sales of council houses are, at present, not clearly seen within the framework of an overall strategy and it will not be until they submit their housing strategies and housing investment programmes later this year that such a picture will begin to emerge. The Government therefore propose to let the general consent to the sale of council houses stand as it is for the time being, but will consider whether the form of the general consent should be amended in the light of the authorities' emerging strategies and investment programmes and rate of sales.

11.40   In view of the public expenditure advantages which would be obtained, the Government also propose to consider with the local authority representatives and the Building Societies Association the scope for a greater flow of building society mortgages to finance the purchase of council houses where they do take place, as well as for 'intermediate' forms of tenure and building for sale.

CHAPTER 12

Individual Housing Needs

12.01   There are quite large numbers of people who may face special difficulties in getting suitable housing. They include:

—lower income households

—homeless people

—one parent families

—battered women

—the physically disabled

—the mentally ill and mentally handicapped

—old people

—single people

—mobile workers

—ethnic minorities.

In the last analysis, the effectiveness of any national housing policy and local housing strategy is likely to be judged by how far it helps those facing the most pressing housing problems.

12.02   The groups listed above overlap. Many people in most of them may find no great difficulty in getting the sort of housing they need. Others may find their problems reduced by the measures discussed in previous chapters for widensng the way into home ownership and public sector tenancies, for increasing the supply of some types of private lettings and for developing new forms of tenure. Those who do face real difficulties in getting suitable housing will often have problems that go much wider than housing. They need concerted help, through central Government policies, and through services provided locally by different departments of a local authority or by co-operation between different authorities. In such cases, the provision of suitable housing is only a part of the jigsaw.

LOWER INCOME HOUSEHOLDERS

12.03   The problem of low income cuts across any method of grouping people in discussion of particular housing problems. Income-related assistance for those with low incomes is available in the form of rent rebates (for local authority and new town tenants), rent allowances (for private and housing association tenants), and more generally under the Supplementary Benefit scheme. These forms of assistance help to ensure that no-one is denied access to adequate rented housing because his income is not enough for him to meet the costs.

12.04   There is no support for home owners directly comparable with rent rebates and allowances, although Supplementary Benefit payments can cover interest charges on mortgages and other essential current expenditure on housing.

12.05 For the reasons discussed in Chapter 5 the Government think it right to continue with some form of housing assistance for tenants which is related to income and to the housing expenses of individual families. The present rent rebate and allowance schemes take account of household income levels, differences in family needs, and varying rent levels. Special concessions are made in areas where rents are exceptionally high. Local authorities have some discretion to make extra payments in special cases.

12.06 The schemes face the same difficulties as other forms of income-related assistance. One is the general problem of the poverty trap. This is perhaps less acute with the rent assistance schemes than with many other income-related schemes, because of the gentle taper of the eligibility limits.

12.07 A special difficulty for some people who are eligible for the rent rebate and rent allowance schemes is the 'better-off' problem. Certain tenants not in full-time work can claim either Supplementary Benefit or rent rebates/allowances; and because of the different bases on which the schemes are operated the balance of advantage between them changes from time to time. Changes are not made more frequently than necessary and tenants on Supplementary Benefit are made aware of their rights. Even so the system continues to cause confusion to tenants and extra administrative expense to the authorities concerned.

12.08 Take-up is also a problem. The record for rent rebates is comparatively good—about 80 per cent at the latest estimate. This is no doubt partly because rents are charged and rebates granted by the same authority. Take-up of rent allowances is much lower—about 35 per cent for unfurnished tenants and probably lower for furnished tenants, although a higher proportion of tenants with larger entitlements do in fact claim them.

12.09 These problems, and the scope and coverage of the rent assistance schemes and their relationship with the Supplementary Benefit scheme, are under review. The Supplementary Benefit Review, announced by the Secretary of State for Social Services in September 1976, is also relevant. But there are two comparatively minor changes to rent assistance schemes which can be made without awaiting the outcome of these reviews, although legislation will be necessary.

12.10 At present Exchequer subsidy meets 100 per cent of the cost of rent allowances but 75 per cent of the cost of rent rebates—the rest is met by the local authorities. The Government propose in future to contribute 90 per cent of the cost of both rebates and allowances. In the case of rent rebates this will particularly help those authorities in hard pressed areas for whom the burden of meeting 25 per cent of the cost has been considerable. It has been argued that the figure should be 100 per cent, on the ground that this is a form of income support for which central Government should take complete responsibility. But an element of local responsibility exists in the assessment of incomes and in the setting of rents which attract rebates. In the case of rent allowances local authorities are responsible for administration of the scheme and for the assessment of incomes, though not for the setting of rents. A 90 per cent contribution for both rebates and allowances seems to the Government a fair compromise. The Government also propose to end the current arrangements under which local authorities pay the Department of Health and Social Security the cost of rent rebates and allowances attributable to tenants in receipt of Supplementary Benefit. They believe that the administrative costs are not justified.

HOMELESSNESS

12.11 Returns made to the Department of the Environment under a new system of statistics instituted in London in 1974, and elsewhere in 1975, confirmed that homelessness is largely concentrated in the inner areas of the major conurbations, particularly London. The statistics largely exclude single people and childless couples. But they show that in 1975 roughly 50,000 homeless households approached local authorities in England for help; some 34,000 were accepted as homeless by authorities and 28,000 found or were provided with permanent accommodation. Others were provided with temporary accommodation whilst awaiting a more permanent answer to their problems.

12.12 The main reason for homelessness among those helped by authorities was domestic disputes (39 per cent of cases). Other causes included repossession by landlords (12 per cent), rent arrears (7 per cent) and—outside London—loss of tied accommodation or mortgage default.

12.13. The statistics also showed that the great majority of homeless people are not newly arrived in an area and that homelessness is a special risk for one-parent families.

12.14 We cannot eliminate all the circumstances that lead to homelessness. But we can take more effective action to deal with homelessness when it occurs. The nature of the help that homeless people require will vary considerably. Some people will be able to make arrangements for themselves with relatively little assistance. For others, particularly in the large crowded conurbations, the problem is overwhelming. The Government are therefore concerned that practical help of some kind should be available to all homeless people from local authorities.

12.15 Responsibility for helping homeless people has often been fragmented. The only clear statutory provision on homelessness—in the National Assistance Act 1948—requires social services authorities to make arrangements to provide temporary accommodation for those in urgent need of it, but it has become increasingly recognised that homelessness must be seen as a housing problem.

12.16 The Government have made it clear that the primary responsibility for assisting homeless people with accommodation should rest with local housing authorities as part of their housing functions. The Housing (Homeless Persons) Bill now before Parliament will give effect to this by transferring responsibility from social services authorities to local housing authorities.

12.17 Social services staff will continue to have an important part to play in helping people who are homeless or threatened with homelessness. But the ending of divided responsibility for housing provision should prove to be a big step forward in dealing with problems of homelessness.

ONE PARENT FAMILIES

12.18 The Report of the Finer Committee on One-Parent Families (1974) drew attention to the housing difficulties faced by single parents, particularly women whose husbands had died or who were divorced or separated. The Committee estimated that in 1971 there were 620,000 one parent families with a total of just over a million dependent children in Great Britain. Over 500,000 of these families were fatherless. A third of families accepted as homeless are one parent families, though one parent families make up only a tenth of all families.

12.19 A very high proportion of one parent families share their home, usually with close relatives. Many are in private rented accommodation, particularly furnished accommodation in inner city areas. They are often living in housing without basic amenities, and in overcrowded conditions. Among some ethnic groups the problems are particularly acute.

12.20 Many single parents find another partner after a time. But until this happens, they can face a period of great difficulty. Mothers whose husbands have left them may face special problems. Local authority tenancies are often in the name of the husband. Many authorities will only transfer the tenancy to the wife after a separation order or divorce. A wife may become caught in a vicious circle if a local authority will not transfer the tenancy to her unless she has a custody order for the children, and a court will not grant custody unless she can demonstrate that she has secure accommodation. Problems can also arise where a wife living in a mortgaged home is deserted by her husband, and he defaults on mortgage payments. In such cases, a building society may allow wives to remain in their home until alternative arrangements are made, by agreeing to accept payments of interest only; and the Supplementary Benefits Commission will accept that the woman is responsible for these payments even though the defaulting husband is the legal owner.

12.21 One parent families may find it difficult to obtain local authority housing because they tend to move frequently and cannot fulfil residence qualifications. Local authorities' points systems can also put one parent families at a disadvantage if—with fewer adults—they get less points than two parent families. The proposal for ending of public rented sector residential qualifications, and the introduction of less rigid allocation policies, would help by making it possible to take full account of individual circumstances (see paragraph 9.21).

12.22 The Government will be issuing guidance to local authorities on the housing problems of one parent families; and the Building Societies Association have agreed to consider giving further guidance to their members.

BATTERED WOMEN

12.23 The Domestic Violence and Matrimonial Proceedings Act 1976, which came into operation on 1 June 1977, makes it possible for a woman to remain in the family home after a household breaks down as a result of domestic violence. It makes it easier for a spouse to get an injunction restraining the other partner from violence or excluding the other partner from the family home. It also provides the police with powers of arrest for breach of an injunction.

12.24 But there is no more urgent or desperate housing problem than that of the woman who is physically assaulted and is forced to flee the marital home. She faces all the problems of other one parent families, and may have to leave suddenly, with her children, without knowing where else she can go. The Government welcome the attention focussed on the needs of this group, particularly by the work of the Select Committee on Violence in Marriage whose report was published in September 1975. The Government's response to the Select Committee's report (Cmnd 6690) drew attention to the immediate need of a woman in such circumstances for some form of shelter while she takes stock of her position and considers what step to take next. For some this can be, and often is, best provided in the home of relations or friends; but for others this sanctuary is not available.

12.25 Since the first refuge opened in 1972 there has been an increasing number and spread of women's aid groups throughout the country specialising in provision of shelter at short notice and offering counselling. There are now some 120 refuges and more are being opened. But women's aid groups encounter many problems in finding properties suitable for use as refuges, and in meeting the costs of essential repairs, conversion, renovation, and maintenance. Prolonged residence in unsatisfactory temporary accommodation can drive women back home despite the risk of further violence. Adequate second-stage and permanent accommodation is needed to release places in refuges for new arrivals who require immediate shelter and support in an emergency. The period a woman will need to spend in a refuge will clearly vary. So too will the subsequent housing help she needs.

12.26 The Government welcome the recognition of this special problem in the Housing (Homeless Persons) Bill. They will shortly be asking authorities for information about the scale of the problem in their area and the nature of the response they have so far been able to make to it. The Government's response to the Select Committee's Report also pointed to ways in which housing authorities can help, principally by making accommodation available for use by voluntary groups, with the help of housing subsidy. They will encourage local authorities to do all they can to deal with this problem.

THE PHYSICALLY DISABLED

12.27 A national survey in 1968 estimated that about 3 million adults in Great Britain were in some degree physically disabled. A great majority were over 50. The housing needs of many of the physically disabled are no different from the general body of the population since the nature of their disablement does not affect the type of housing they need.

12.28 Most physically disabled people would like to go on living in their own homes, among friends and in a familiar neighbourhood. The greater the degree of disablement, the more necessary it is that effective domiciliary assistance should be provided by the health and social service authorities. But their housing must be physically suitable also. Some of the physically disabled need special features such as ramped access, handrails, a downstairs W.C., which can be provided by adaptation of existing houses. A minority however need specially designed houses.

12.29 In 1974 the Government started a drive to get more done for the physically disabled. They provided special improvement grants allowing for adaptations to private sector housing under the Housing Act 1974. The Government have also recently indicated their willingness to contemplate a change in this Act, giving local authorities a discretion, in cases of hardship, to waive the rateable value limits—which are a feature of the improvement grant scheme —where disabled people are affected. Local authorities carrying out adaptations to their own stock receive housing subsidy. Local authority social service departments may also provide help to physically disabled people for adaptation of both public and private sector houses, though the Government have proposed that primary responsibility for public sector adaptations should be transferred to housing authorities.

12.30 As for specially designed new housing, the Government have sought to stimulate greater efforts by private developers. But clearly the major responsibility must continue to rest with the public rented sector. The Government have therefore fostered a programme of new building directed to the needs of the physically disabled, and have assisted local authorities and housing associations through the subsidy system and design guidance. There are two basic designs:

—*mobility housing*, which is 'Parker Morris' housing from which steps have been eliminated and in which doorways have been widened; and

—*wheelchair housing* for those who spend all their time in a wheelchair, and which contains greater circulation space and wheelchair aids.

12.31 Though much more needs to be done, the Government have been encouraged by the recent response from public rented sector authorities. Over 2,000 wheelchair units have been built since the passing of the Chronically Sick and Disabled Persons Act of 1970; and over 11,000 mobility units have either been built or have been put into the pipeline since the Government urged greater provision of this type of special housing in 1974.

12.32 The Government will continue to encourage greater provision of housing for physically disabled people; and more effective co-ordination between housing and social services departments and the health service at central and local level.

THE MENTALLY ILL AND MENTALLY HANDICAPPED

12.33 Local housing authorities, housing associations, and new towns can play a valuable part in the recovery of the mentally ill and in helping many of the mentally handicapped to lead reasonably independent lives, by working with local social services departments to find ways of solving problems of accommodation.

12.34 Some of the mentally ill and handicapped will inevitably need the specialist residential accommodation provided by the social services. But this is frequently not the case. What is often required is essentially ordinary housing. For example, a housing authority can provide cluster flats or bedsitter accommodation, with any necessary support coming from the social services; or the housing authority can provide ordinary flats and houses to serve as group homes, with social services again providing support. People who need the mutual support of living together in a small group can sometimes live as one household.

OLD PEOPLE

12.35 In 1975 there were nearly 7 million people aged 65 or over (2·5 million over 75) in England and Wales—14 per cent of the total population. Between 1961 and 1975 the total population grew by $6\frac{1}{2}$ per cent; the over 65s increased by almost 27 per cent. Between 1975 and 1986 a further increase of 450,000 ($6\frac{1}{2}$ per cent) is expected in the number of people aged 65 and over; but for people aged 75 and over the increase is put at 570,000 (23 per cent.) This is one of the most significant of contemporary demographic trends.

12.36 Most elderly people already live in the community; only about 5 per cent are in hospital or in residential and nursing homes. The Government's policy is to enable elderly people to remain in the community as long as possible and to go on living full and independent lives. The Government are therefore giving high priority within available resources to the development of domiciliary health and personal social services and to the encouragement of other means of preventing or postponing the need for long-term care in hospital or residential homes. The level of development of the various domiciliary services in any one area will depend on local circumstances, but the services are available to all old people living in the community, irrespective of the kind of housing they occupy.

12.37 Many elderly people live in substandard housing. In 1971 a quarter of all elderly households lacked the exclusive use of one or more of the basic amenities. The older the household the fewer the amenities, and the more likely it is that the accommodation itself is old. The changes in improvement policy discussed in Chapter 10 should help many old people.

12.38 Furthermore some elderly people will require housing more suitable to their needs. This may vary from ordinary small accommodation—some of it built to mobility standards—to specially designed housing with a resident warden. This range of more suitable housing for old people is being provided mainly by local authorities or housing associations. Residential care on a permanent basis is normally provided by local authority social service departments (under Part III of the National Assistance Act 1948) only where elderly persons cannot manage on their own in the community, even with domiciliary support, and do not need hospital care. In 1976 there were some 115,000 places available in local authority residential homes for old people.

12.39 No figures are available for the numbers in public rented sector sheltered housing. The last survey was carried out in 1965, when there were about 65,000 elderly people in such housing in England and Wales. Since 1969, when the Government issued standards for sheltered housing on the lines of grouped flatlets embodying a variety of communal facilities and a warden, as well as for self-contained accommodation, local authorities and housing associations have done more and more to meet the needs of the elderly. Between 1974 and 1976 more than 25 per cent (80,000) of all local authority houses completed in England and Wales were specially designed for the elderly.

12.40   The proposed abolition of local authority residential qualifications—discussed in Chapter 9—will help elderly people who have to move and would benefit from local authority accommodation—for example those who have had to give up homes on going into hospital, or who have previously lived in tied houses, or those who wish to move to live near relatives, perhaps in 'granny annexes'. Housing associations are supplementing the work of many local authorities in helping the elderly to move out of large property by providing them with alternative accommodation. This can often release housing which is itself suitable for conversion into smaller units for old people.

12.41   The implementation of Government policy on the care of the elderly depends upon local housing authorities being fully involved with health and social service authorities in establishing effective methods of assessing need, planning provision, providing facilities and allocating resources. There is considerable scope for fuller co-operation in planning service developments in the three fields and for co-ordination of administrative policies—for example admission and discharge procedures in hospital and residential homes, and tenancy allocation procedures for housing. Local decisions have to be taken on the balance between the various forms of special and sheltered housing provision and residential accommodation, on the type of facilities and on staffing to be provided in sheltered housing, and on the support to be provided by domiciliary services.

12.42   The Government will be issuing comprehensive guidance on these and other issues involved in making adequate provision for the elderly in the years ahead, based on a 1976 consultation paper and the response to it.

SINGLE PEOPLE

12.43   There are now about 8½ million single people of working age in England and Wales. Many are content to share as part of larger households, usually their families. But there is a rising trend of one-person households among men and women of working age—the figure for 1961 in England and Wales was about ¾ million; the estimate for 1976 is over 1·3 million. The figures contain a growing number of young single households: 70,000 under 30 in 1961; 275,000 under 30 in 1976. There is not much doubt that more and more single people would like a 'place of their own' if they can find and afford it. This applies of course not only to young people at work but to young people in further education—students and apprentices.

12.44   In 1971 4 per cent of home owners were men and women of working age living alone. Their access to this sector is limited by financial and institutional constraints. Saving for a down-payment on one wage is difficult, and some building societies are particularly cautious about lending on the types of property which single people tend to prefer.

12.45 Only 4 per cent of local authority tenants in 1971 were men and women of working age living alone. Many authorities will not admit them to waiting lists at all, while others make registration conditional upon age.

12.46 Single people have traditionally looked to the private rented sector for accommodation—35 per cent of all private furnished rented accommodation was occupied by single people below pensionable age in 1971. But the private rented sector has been declining for many years. And the decline of cheap lodging houses and hostels has thrown up special problems—in 1972 there were 17 per cent fewer beds than in 1965—which tend to be at their worst in the inner areas of the large cities.

12.47 The needs of many single people—whether working or in full-time education—may often not be as pressing as for example those of a family with small children living in an unfit house or in overcrowded conditions. But their problems are nevertheless real enough, and some are living in difficult circumstances.

12.48 Single people—according to their age and situation—should benefit from the various measures proposed in previous chapters for increasing the supply of and access to housing:

—More helpful forms of mortgage facilities for first-time house buyers (Chapter 7) will be available to single people as well as other house buyers.

—Digs and lodgings have been a traditional form of accommodation for single people. They should therefore benefit if local authorities in general allow tenants to take in lodgers (see paragraph 11.10). They also stand to gain from the measures described in Chapter 8, to encourage more letting by resident private landlords and to bring empty flats over shops back into use.

—More flexible local authority allocation policies (Chapter 9) will also help, not only in areas where demand is reducing, but in other areas where some kinds of property are difficult to let to families with children. Official surveys, and the Greater London Council's experience of making 'difficult-to-let' property available to single people and childless couples, have revealed a considerable hidden demand for suitable public rented sector accommodation.

—Development of intermediate forms of tenure (Chapter 11).

Continuing co-operation between local authorities, housing associations and voluntary bodies to improve the quality of hostel accommodation can also benefit the single.

12.49 The Government also consider that, subject to availability of resources, local authorities should ensure that adequate accommodation for single people is included in their general investment provision for small houses. The Government have accepted that where the presence of students adds to housing pressures, local authorities and housing associations may receive subsidy or grant for providing accommodation for single people which is to be let primarily to students.

MOBILE WORKERS

12.50 Industry, the economy, and workers and their families would all benefit if it were easier for people to move house to places where there are jobs to suit them. There is already a fair measure of mobility. In 1971, 35 per cent of households had moved at least once during the previous 5 years. But there are wide variations. For example, those in higher socio-economic groups or with higher incomes tend to move more often; and whereas moves by home owners and local authority tenants are roughly equal in total, mobility between regions is much more common among home owners than local authority tenants. These differences suggest that more could be done to facilitate mobility for all members of the community.

12.51 Local authorities can do a lot to help. They have a strategic role through their planning responsibilities and local housing strategies. They can help to foster mobility, especially in inner city areas, by seeking to achieve a better balance between housing and employment. In assessing housing need they should try to identify the desirable scale of mobility, especially in respect of skilled workers. They should formulate proposals accordingly, for example by trying to see that houses are made available—if needs be by themselves—for letting or for sale at the right time and in the right places in relation to jobs.

12.52 The way local authorities allocate their stock can also have an important effect on mobility. Further guidance will be given when the Housing Services Advisory Group has completed its study of allocation policy and practices, but it is already clear that the abandonment of residential qualifications would help freer movement of labour. Providing houses for in-comers with good employment reasons for entering the area can make all the difference to the families concerned and can equally help a local firm to survive and prosper. Conditions of access imposed by some local authorities such as 'date order and merit schemes' act as a damper on both job and housing prospects for many individuals.

12.53 Local authorities can also improve their arrangements for transfers and exchanges both within and between local authority areas. This is of special importance in the whole of the Greater London area.

12.54 Several of the policies advocated elsewhere in this Green Paper—including those listed in paragraph 12.48 in relation to single people—will help mobile families. In particular, they will benefit from:

—the promotion of home ownership, including proposals for assisting first-time house-buyers and for securing a reasonably stable flow of mortgage funds so that home owners who want to move are not left high and dry by mortgage famines;

—the continued promotion of housing association provision and the encouragement of new forms of tenure. Some housing associations are already helping to meet the needs of mobile workers. Co-ownership and equity sharing schemes can also make a special contribution to mobility while making fewer demands than rented schemes on resources required to meet other priority housing needs.

ETHNIC MINORITIES

12.55 Ethnic minorities have benefited and will continue to benefit from policies designed to help all those in housing need. The Government's 1975 White Paper 'Race Relations and Housing' (Cmnd 6232) emphasised that housing is pre-eminently a service in which the main contribution towards helping coloured people is made through general programmes and policies, providing for common requirements which have nothing to do with colour. But it is a fact that a higher proportion of households of New Commonwealth origin live in poor housing conditions, especially as regards overcrowding and lack of exclusive use of amenities.

12.56 Members of ethnic minorities who become home owners often buy cheaper older houses. Survey results published in 1976* showed that in 1974 84 per cent of Asian householders who were semi-skilled and unskilled manual workers were home owners. Because of their low incomes, the quality of their houses and the areas in which they lived tended to be poor. The same survey found that low income also led to heavy reliance on local authority mortgages: 39 per cent of West Indian and 33 per cent of Asian owner-occupiers obtained their mortgage in this way, compared with 13 per cent of other home owners in the sample. When local authority lending for house-purchase is restricted, such potential house-buyers may be helped through the 'support' lending arrangements with the building societies. Otherwise, they may be compelled to use fringe finance houses and money lenders charging very high interest rates. But the measures proposed in Chapter 7 for an expansion of building society lending to people with modest incomes and on the purchase of older cheaper property, within the framework of local housing strategies, should help with these difficulties.

12.57 Ethnic minorities also face extra problems in gaining access to local authority housing. These include lack of knowledge of local authority housing; an inability to meet residential qualifications; and size of family (because local authorities have comparatively few dwellings with 4 or more bedrooms, large families have to wait longer for accommodation). Ethnic minorities have tended to receive less desirable local authority accommodation. One reason for this is that a relatively high proportion apply to local authorities when they are faced with homelessness and so cannot afford to wait for better accommodation to become available.

12.58 Homelessness among young black people, especially where compounded by unemployment and alienation, is an especially severe problem in some inner city areas. Accommodation for these young people is an important step towards

*D. J. Smith: "The Facts of Racial Disadvantage" (PEP, 1976)

dealing with their problems. Direct involvement of the black community is more likely to achieve success than solutions imposed from above—for example, some authorities have leased houses to self-help groups with this in mind.

12.59 The Government will continue to ensure that these and other special problems faced by ethnic minorities are taken fully into account in the development of housing policies and programmes, in consultation with the new Commission for Racial Equality. This is an issue which must be faced up to both by public sector authorities providing rented housing, and by building societies and others lending for house purchase.

CHAPTER 13

The Inner City

13.01 The last chapter considered—within the framework of the national housing policy—how special housing problems that sometimes confront *individuals* might be tackled. But *places* can have housing problems of a special character too, when there are concentrations of bad housing conditions. These problems are intensified when they are found—as they commonly are— alongside other economic and social difficulties. This is particularly true of the inner city areas.

13.02 The recent White Paper on policy for the inner cities (Cmnd 6845) promised a new and sustained attack on the social and economic problems of the inner city areas. In order to concentrate attention and resources on cities where the problems are at their worst, partnership arrangements between central and local government are being offered in the first instance to Liverpool, Birmingham, Manchester/Salford, and in London—where many inner city problems exist in a severe form and on a unique scale—to Lambeth and the Docklands. The Government have made it clear that the chief instrument for change in the inner city must be the main programmes and policies of central and local authorities. No programme has a more important part to play than housing.

13.03 Inner city areas have no monopoly of housing problems. But they have more than their share, and these problems are associated with other disadvantages, among them unemployment, low income, poor social facilities, and vandalism. The local authorities concerned have made great efforts to cope with post-war housing problems but have not always had the success that their energies deserved. Looking back, some of the reasons seem to be:

—Large-scale slum clearance and redevelopment programmes have been a major instrument of change. In many places there was no alternative: the conditions were too bad for anything else. But these programmes have often taken a long time, sapped confidence, disrupted communities, swept away much-needed jobs in small firms, and failed to produce a satisfactory new environment.

—Too little emphasis has been placed upon rehabilitation, repair and better use of existing houses.

—In addition, we can now see that the building of large areas of new housing has created new problems. Many inner areas contain estates built in the nineteen thirties and nineteen fifties where the houses and flats may be physically adequate, in the sense that they have all the basic amenities, but are drab, poorly serviced and ill-maintained. They leave no place for individuality; they often stand in dreary and anonymous surroundings, short of play areas and other social facilities; they can become 'dump' estates. People who live there are keen to get away, and it is hard to persuade others to take their place.

—Opportunities for choosing between types of home and tenure have narrowed. Large-scale redevelopment has produced too many high-rise flats in some neighbourhoods. The old owner-occupied houses have not been

120

replaced as land and building costs and relatively cheap transport between city centres and suburbs have made it more attractive to build elsewhere. The private rented sector has continued to contract.

—Both central and local government have sometimes adopted a rigid and bureaucratic approach to inner area redevelopment, failing to adapt and modify programmes to take account of the facts of the local situation and the wishes of the people affected.

13.04   Inner areas do not all have the same housing problems. In some, over-crowding is the dominant issue; in others, the poor condition of old houses. In some inner areas there are shortages of housing land; in others, tracts of dereliction. Even within the same city neighbouring communities may suffer in quite different ways. There are significant variations within the 'partnership cities' as well as between them, although all have housing problems which add to the collective deprivation of their residents.

London

13.05   Despite declining household numbers, London is still the city of the greatest housing stress. Unlike England and Wales as a whole, which has more houses than households (about 3 per cent of the stock), there is only a rough balance in London before taking into account necessary vacancies (see paragraphs 3.04–3.12). Many households still live in poor conditions—London had the largest percentage of households sharing and the highest percentage of overcrowding at the time of the 1971 Census. London therefore still exhibits many of the difficulties associated with housing shortage.

13.06   London's housing problems are mainly to be found in its inner areas. In some boroughs, such as Lambeth, there is overcrowding and a shortage of housing, and at the same time under-occupation and some empty houses. Much of the housing in inner London was built before the First World War, and many of these houses are now in need of rehabilitation. Throughout inner London some of the local authority estates built since 1945, to replace the houses lost in the Second World War and to ease pressing housing shortages, have given rise to their own management and social problems. In Docklands, where there are large areas of land in disuse, redevelopment for housing or for other purposes will present difficulties.

13.07   Mobility in the public sector is low because each of the 32 London boroughs has its own waiting list, and usually only those who have already lived in the borough for a specified period can get on to the waiting list. The Greater London Council and the housing associations help to ease the problem, since they allocate their houses on different criteria, but the lack of a flexible and co-ordinated allocation system hinders the best use of the housing stock. Much of inner London's housing stock is still in the private rented sector, but the continuing decline of the sector has increased the problems facing its traditional customers. Homelessness is the grimmest aspect of housing stress; and inner London has the greatest number of homeless people in the country.

13.08   The actions of the London authorities and of private sector house-builders over the past 30 years have greatly reduced the capital's housing pro-blems, particularly the numerical shortage—even though the problem of poor

121

housing conditions is still very great. But the progress achieved in the public sector has imposed substantial burdens on General Rate Funds and on the Exchequer. One reason is the size of the programme; another is the relatively high cost of land and building in London (particularly in inner London, where there are no easy sites); a third is the rent and management policies that some authorities have adopted. The Action Group on London Housing—a group convened for joint discussion by central and local government of London's housing problems—has drawn attention to the costs arising from the relatively long time taken by many London authorities to develop housing sites. The cost-effectiveness of public sector housing is an important issue for the London housing authorities.

13.09 It is widely accepted that inner London's housing needs cannot be met by action in the inner boroughs alone. Investment in outer London, where costs are less prohibitive and where there is more land suitable for house building, must contribute to the solution. The aim must be to produce a strategy, not only for each authority but for London as a whole, which ensures that investment is cost-effective and gives it the right balance between areas, between the public and private sectors, between forms of tenure, and between new building and projections. The Department of the Environment's proposed Housing Survey should provide a more accurate picture of London than can be got from the 1971 census data (see paragraph 3.03).

Other Cities

13.10 The range of inner area housing problems is well illustrated in the other cities where the Government have so far proposed partnerships. Birmingham (like Lambeth) has overcrowding in the inner areas. Because there are few large areas of building land in the centre the City authorities are concentrating new development on smaller sites. They have also adopted a policy of redevelopment and improvement of the existing poor housing in General Improvement Areas and Housing Action Areas. Most of the 80,000 houses in Liverpool built before 1919 are in the inner area of the City, and they are mainly in private ownership. Many privately rented houses are overcrowded and in poor repair. Past slum clearance programmes and planning blight have left extensive parts of inner Liverpool's land vacant. Some local authority housing in the inner areas is overcrowded and heavily vandalised, with many dwellings proving difficult to let. Despite extensive slum clearance and rebuilding programmes since the nineteen fifties, the inner areas of Manchester and Salford contain 60,000 dwellings in need of treatment, mainly improvement. Salford still has a major slum clearance problem, but the City of Manchester has now been able to reduce its clearance programme to about 500 houses a year. Like Liverpool, both cities have above average proportions of privately rented dwellings, and Manchester also has considerable numbers of difficult-to-let flats in high density development.

Relevance of the housing policy proposals

13.11 The urgent need to make a greater impact on the problems of the inner city areas is one of the major factors which have shaped the proposals for the national housing policy set out in this Green Paper.

13.12 Although there is a great variety of circumstances in the inner cities, five main housing problems stand out:

—run-down housing and shabby neighbourhoods;

—bleak local authority estates;

—a limited choice of tenures;

—disproportionate numbers of people with special housing needs; and

—problems of housing mobility.

13.13 All of these are explicitly covered by discussion of different aspects of the national housing policy in earlier chapters. For example:

—The greater emphasis on gradual renewal, rehabilitation and repair—rather than demolition and rebuilding—should speed progress in dealing with run-down housing in all tenures, and lift morale in neighbourhoods which otherwise might sink into irreversible decline (Chapter 10).

—The recognition of the need for a larger proportion of resources for management and maintenance to go to local authorities with 'problem' estates, and the proposals in the Tenants' Charter to strengthen the rights of tenants and involve them in the running of their estates, should go a long way towards reducing the sense of alienation of many public sector tenants in the inner cities (Chapter 11).

—Wider choice of tenure will be encouraged by measures to assist first time purchasers (Chapter 7); to stimulate the supply of some types of private letting (Chapter 8); to continue to support the housing association movement and extend the range of families catered for by local authorities (Chapter 9); and to encourage new intermediate tenures and building for sale by local authorities (Chapter 11). These measures could help retain younger people and attract back skilled workers to the inner areas.

—Proposals for easing the problem of people with special housing needs—ranging from the homeless, to mobile workers who are crucial for the industrial regeneration of the inner cities—were discussed in Chapter 12.

—The new towns can do more to relieve the problems of inner city areas directly by taking a greater number of elderly, disadvantaged and unskilled people (Chapter 9).

—In general, the new public rented sector housing investment programmes and subsidy arrangements will ensure that inner city areas with severe housing problems will have higher priority in the allocation of capital resources, and that their existing tenants and ratepayers do not have to bear a disproportionate share of the high costs of essential housing investment (Chapter 9).

E

13.14   But although there are some similarities between the inner cities, there are also great differences, as illustrated in paragraphs 13.06 and 13.10. The key to success in dealing with the housing problems of the inner cities will be the local housing strategies discussed in Chapter 6. The development of housing strategies will enable inner city local authorities to tackle the housing needs of their areas across a broad front—as part of a wider strategy for regeneration, involving a better balance between housing and employment—in co-operation with all other public and private bodies concerned.

CHAPTER 14

Summary of Conclusions and Proposals

14.01 The Government's *conclusions on the present situation*, based on the description and analysis in Part II of the Green Paper, are summarised in Chapter 2.

14.02 The Government's *housing objectives*, which take into account the conclusions on the present situation, are set out in paragraph 2.16; and the Government's *proposed national housing policy* for implementing these objectives is outlined in Chapter 6.

14.03 Specific conclusions and proposals put forward in this Green Paper—principally in Part III—are summarised below. They are in the order in which the main references appear in the text, and the numbers in brackets show the paragraphs in which these main references occur:

1. Housing surveys. A National Housing Survey and a survey of vacant dwellings will be launched later this year (3.03).

2. DOE Housing Unit. The Department of the Environment intend to establish a special Unit to analyse information about housing and to monitor progress (3.03).

3. Tax relief. Tax relief on mortgage interest and option mortgage subsidy will continue. The limit of £25,000 on the part of loans for house purchase admissible for tax relief will be kept under review (5.30–5.38).

4. Local housing strategies. Local authorities will be asked to prepare comprehensive local housing strategies. The strategies will be based on assessments of the full range of housing needs in each area, taking account of policies in other fields—such as transport and employment, health and social services—within the broad framework of development plans. Local housing strategies will involve a wide variety of action in both public and private sectors, and will call for further development of existing working relationships between local authorities and all other bodies concerned with housing in their areas, such as the Housing Corporation, registered housing associations, local housebuilders, building societies, new town corporations, county councils, and tenants' and community organisations (6.03–6.10).

5. Consultation with local authority representatives. A Housing Consultative Council for England will be established, under the chairmanship of the Secretary of State for the Environment, to consider all major issues of concern to local authorities in the performance of their housing duties. Existing consultative machinery involving other bodies concerned with housing, such as the building societies and housebuilders, will be maintained. In Wales, the existing relationship with the Council of the Principality will be developed (6.11).

6. Low-start mortgages. Building societies should make low-start mortgages more widely available, and in particular offer them to borrowers who select an option mortgage (7.22).

7. *Higher percentage mortgages.* Building societies should make higher percentage loans more readily available. This should be possible now that the Building Societies Association (BSA) have arranged for guarantees to cover such loans to be extended (7.26–7.27).

8. *Loans on older properties.* More building society lending on older properties, including both unimproved and converted properties, will be an essential part of local housing strategies (7.28).

9. *Co-operation between building societies and local authorities.* Experience with support lending has provided a foundation for working partnerships between building societies and local authorities at local level. Local authorities should complement the work of building societies by providing topping-up loans, by providing improvement and repair grants in respect of older houses bought for home ownership, and by guarantees. They should keep building societies informed about their local housing strategies; this should reduce 'red-lining' and help revitalise inner city areas (7.29–7.32).

10. *Special Government assistance for first-time purchasers.* The Government propose, after consulting the institutions concerned, to introduce new savings bonus and loans schemes for first time purchasers. The savings bonus might be broadly equivalent to income tax at the basic rate on the aggregate of interest on up to £1,000 of qualifying savings. The loan—subject to house price limits—would be £500 for each first-time buyer who saved a matching sum under the savings bonus scheme over at least 2 years; it would be interest-free for the first five years (7.33–7.42).

11. *Local authority mortgage rates.* The Government propose to introduce legislation to enable local authorities to charge a mortgage rate equal to that recommended by the BSA, with any deficit or surplus charged or credited to the General Rate Fund (7.43).

12. *Social criteria in mortgage lending.* Within the limits of acceptable and reasonable commercial risks, building societies should give due weight to social factors when deciding what priority to give to applications for mortgages (7.46–7.47).

13. *A stable supply of mortgage funds.* Greater stability in the volume of mortgage lending can be achieved by development of the voluntary arrangements between the Government and the building societies through the Joint Advisory Committee. The building societies should:
   (a) build up their stabilisation 'funds' to higher levels when possible;
   (b) keep their structure of interest rates paid to investors more in line with the market;
   (c) adopt a more flexible relationship between the rate paid by mortgagors and the rate paid to investors;
   (d) be prepared to raise short-term loans on the money market (7.49–7.55).

14. *Government help with stabilisation arrangements.* To avoid losses to building societies resulting from the stabilisation arrangements, the Government

might accept part of the stabilisation funds for investment in the National Loans Fund, subject to agreement on the size of mortgage lending and of stabilisation funds. The Government would also be prepared in exceptional circumstances to consider short-term loans from public funds (7.56).

15. *Size of individual loan for house purchase.* Building societies should extend the practice of requiring an existing mortgagor to 'plough back' net proceeds of the sale of an existing house into the purchase of the next, so that available mortgage funds can be spread among a larger number of borrowers (7.60).

16. *Fresh sources of mortgage funds.* The case for a special financial intermediary, to raise funds from institutions—in particular life and pension funds—and on-lend them to building societies, might be considered. Such an agency could also help with raising short-term loans to stabilise the flow of funds to societies. The intermediary could be a public or private body, but the building societies may prefer to develop any necessary machinery themselves (7.61–7.64).

17. *Building society quotas for housebuilders.* Further development of arrangements to stabilise the flow of mortgage funds should enable building societies to go further in providing advance mortgage 'quotas' for housebuilders (7.66).

18. *Housing land.* In fulfilling their duties under the Community Land Act, local authorities must have regard to the housebuilders' need for a steady supply of land (7.67).

19. *Private rented sector.* The Government are studying the problems of the private rented sector in detail in the separate Review of the Rent Acts. Their main conclusions should be announced by the end of the year. But it is already clear that the following three measures could help to alleviate the problems created by the sector's contraction (8.15).

20. *Letting by resident private landlords.* Letting by resident landlords and temporarily absent home owners should be encouraged by speeding up the procedures for obtaining repossession (8.19–8.21).

21. *Accommodation normally let with a business.* Lettings of flats over shops and other accommodation normally let with a business should not in future attract full security of tenure (8.22).

22. *A publicly accountable letting agency in the private rented sector.* The terms on which new private investment might be attracted into a publicly accountable letting agency should be explored (8.23).

23. *Housing Investment Programmes.* Local authorities in England will be asked to draw up housing investment programmes—related to their local housing strategy—covering their own capital expenditure for the coming 4 years on clearance and demolition, renovation, conversion, home loans, improvement grants to private householders, acquisition, and new building.

The Government will make capital spending allocations to each authority on the basis of their plans. A similar approach will be developed in Wales (9.06–9.10).

24. Cost control of local authority housebuilding. A new method of cost control for local authority housebuilding, based on a fixed level of costs eligible for subsidy, instead of the present housing cost yardstick, will be developed in consultation with local authorities (9.11).

25. Local authority housing accounts. The Government will discuss with local authorities new forms of accounts to assist effective financial management, and will explore the case for reintroducing statutory repairs accounts, linked with a new subsidy system (9.11).

26. Types of housing. Local housing and planning authorities will need to ensure within the overall local housing strategy that requirements for widely differing types of housing are met (9.12–9.14).

27. Public sector housing standards. The Department of the Environment and the Welsh Office will consult local authority representatives about the scope for introducing greater flexibility into public sector ('Parker Morris') housing standards (9.15).

28. Local authority allocation policies. Local authorities will be encouraged to liberalise their allocation policies to embrace a wider range of needs (9.16–9.19).

29. Qualifications for entry to local authority waiting lists. The Government will consider the case for legislation to prohibit residential or other qualifications for entry to local authority waiting lists (9.21).

30. Publication of local authority allocation schemes. The Government will introduce legislation requiring allocation schemes to be published (9.22).

31. The role of housing associations. The role of registered housing associations should continue to grow and be integrated in local housing strategies. Housing associations should normally publish their allocation schemes (9.25–9.26).

32. New towns. New towns need to house increasing numbers of the elderly and disadvantaged people who are willing to move from the inner cities. They should also be prepared to meet the growing demand for home ownership (9.28–9.29).

33. Local authority subsidies. The present subsidy arrangements should be replaced by a system which will effectively bridge the gap between reasonable costs and a reasonable contribution from local sources, while leaving local authorities their present freedom to fix rents and make Rate Fund contributions (9.34).

34. Local authority rents. The proposed subsidy system will enable the balance between central and local contributions to housing costs to be struck in the light of all relevant factors, including past and expected movements in incomes, costs and prices. The Government consider that over a run of years rents should keep broadly in line with changes in money incomes (9.37) (see also 5.28–5.29).

35. Rate support grant. The treatment of General Rate Fund contributions for rate support grant purposes will be discussed with local authorities in the light of the proposals in the Green Paper on Local Government Finance (Cmnd 6813) (9.40–9.41).

36. Subsidy 'floor'. The idea of a 'subsidy floor' for individual authorities related to tax relief at the basic rate is put forward for public discussion as a means of achieving a greater sense of fairness between local authority tenants and home owners (9.47–9.50).

37. Loan repayment period. Local authorities will be given greater freedom to vary the loan repayment period for investment without loss of subsidy entitlement (9.56).

38. New town and housing association subsidies. The proposed new local authority subsidy system can be applied to new towns, with appropriate adjustments (9.57). The case for introducing similar arrangements for housing associations, and the arrangements for fixing housing association rents, will be considered in consultation with the Housing Corporation and the National Federation of Housing Associations (9.59–9.61).

39. A change of emphasis in renovation policy. Work on the renovation of older houses should be directed more at bringing larger numbers of houses up to a decent basic standard rather than on higher standard improvements of a smaller number of houses (10.19–10.20).

40. More flexible administration of improvement grants. The Government will encourage a less rigid approach to the administration of improvement grants in order to stimulate improvements to a basic standard (10.22–10.23).

41. Repairs grants. 'Repairs only' grants will be made more widely available (10.24–10.25).

42. Cost and rateable value limits on improvement grants. Consideration will be given to increases in existing cost and rateable value limits for improvement grants (10.26).

43. Improvement grants for private tenants. The Government will examine the possibility of allowing private tenants to apply for grants towards the improvement of the houses they occupy, with no increase in rent resulting from the improvement to the property (10.28) (see also *54* below).

44. Repair and improvement grants for houses in multiple occupation. Grant will be made available towards the cost of repairs to houses in multiple occupation, as for other houses (10.30). Consideration will be given to the introduction of mandatory grants towards the cost of installation of basic amenities for houses in multiple occupation (10.31).

45. Compulsory improvements. Local authorities' powers to compel improvement and repair of unsatisfactory houses will be examined with a view to making them simpler and more effective (10.32).

46. Removal of ban on payment of grant to home owners in formerly rented houses. Provision will be made to remove the present ban on payment of improvement grants to owner-occupiers of houses in special areas which have been let within the preceding 12 months (10.33).

47. The choice between renovation and new building. Local authorities will be given further economic advice on methods of appraising the advantages of renovation or new building which take account of the full range of resources involved. Social costs and benefits, which often favour rehabilitation, should also be taken into account (10.36–10.37).

48. Empty private houses. Government procedures for dealing with compulsory purchase orders on empty houses will be speeded up. Local authorities should consider taking more leases of empty privately owned houses (10.40).

49. Vacancy periods in local authority houses. Local authorities should reduce vacancy periods within their own stock to a minimum, and should review existing procedures with this in mind (10.40).

50. Better use of the housing stock. Local authorities can improve the use of the housing stock by such measures as subdivision of older houses, increased direct provision of smaller houses, and 'movement incentives' for local authority tenants to help with transaction costs. The Government will issue a circular giving fuller guidance (10.42–10.43).

51. A Tenants' Charter. A code of principles and practices designed to protect the freedom and rights of public sector tenants will be introduced and consideration will be given to similar improvements in the rights of private tenants (11.06 and 11.18).

52. Security of tenure and right to a written agreement for public sector tenants. Legislation will be introduced to give public sector tenants security of tenure and the right to a written tenancy agreement (11.07).

53. Rights and obligations of public sector tenants. The Department of the Environment will issue guidance on tenancy agreements in the public sector designed to provide a better balance between the rights and obligations of landlords and tenants (11.08).

54. Improvements and sub-letting by public sector tenants. Tenants should be permitted and encouraged to carry out improvements to their homes subject to reimbursement for substantial improvement when the tenancy ends (11.09) and to sub-let rooms (11.10).

55. Management and maintenance. Tenants should be able to expect better management and maintenance of their homes. Consideration is being given to the possibility of a more selective treatment of management and maintenance expenditure in the new subsidy system, to take account of the needs of authorities with problem estates (11.11–11.12).

56. Tenant involvement in management. Tenants should be given a greater say in the running of their estates, and enabled to participate formally or informally in management decisions; such arrangements could be taken a stage further through the formation of housing co-operatives (11.13–11.15).

57. Housing association co-operatives. The Government will continue to encourage the formation of co-operatives in the housing association movement, through its support of the Co-operative Housing Agency, and will legislate to remove obstacles to this policy (11.16–11.17).

58. Co-operative purchase by private tenants. The scope for giving private tenants the right to purchase their homes on a co-operative basis, where blocks are up for sale, will be considered (11.19).

59. Co-ownership housing. The Government intend to revive co-ownership housing. Current legislation will be amended to permit housing associations to build for sale, either outright or on an equity-sharing basis (11.22–11.23).

60. 'Intermediate' forms of tenure. The spread and development of equity-sharing schemes in the local authority and housing association spheres, and of further ventures in 'intermediate' forms of tenure in both private and public sectors, will be encouraged (11.25–11.28).

61. Building for sale by local authorities. In allocating the resources available to them, local authorities should take account of the opportunities to meet housing need by building new houses—and consider the scope for converting or rehabilitating existing houses—for sale or for the newer 'intermediate' forms of tenure (11.30–11.33).

62. Sale of council houses. The Government consider that an authority's proposals to sell should be seen as part of the total approach to housing for its area, including in particular its proposals for meeting demands for rented accommodation of the right type and quality. The general consent to the sale of council houses will be allowed to stand for the present, but will be considered in the light of emerging local strategies, housing investment programmes, and rates of sales (11.34–11.39).

63. Building society funds for council house purchase. The Government propose to consider with the local authority associations and the BSA the scope for greater use of building society mortgages to finance the purchase of council houses, as well as 'intermediate' forms of tenure and building for sale (11.40).

64. Lower income householders. Income-related rent rebates and rent allowances will be continued; the scope and coverage of the present schemes are under review (12.05–12.09).

65. Exchequer contribution to rent assistance schemes. Exchequer subsidy payable on the cost of rent rebates and rent allowances will be standardised at 90 per cent. Reimbursement by local authorities to the Department of Health and Social Security of the cost of rent rebates and allowances in respect of tenants receiving Supplementary Benefit will be ended (12.10).

131

66.   Homelessness.   The Housing (Homeless Persons) Bill now before Parliament should result in a real advance in dealing with problems of homelessness by placing the primary responsibility for this on local housing authorities (12.15–12.17).

67.   One-parent families.   The Government will be issuing guidance to local authorities on the housing of one-parent families; and the BSA have agreed to consider giving further guidance to their members (12.22).

68.   Battered women.   Local authorities will be asked to provide information about the scale of the problem of battered women in their areas, and will be encouraged to help with the provision of accommodation (12.26).

69.   Disabled and handicapped people.   The Government will consider legislative changes giving local authorities discretion to waive rateable value limits for improvement grants where disabled people are affected, and will continue to encourage greater provision of housing for disabled or handicapped people (12.29–12.34).

70.   Old people.   The Government's policy of enabling elderly people to remain in the community as long as possible will be maintained, and comprehensive guidance will be issued on housing and other services for old people (12.35–12.42).

71.   Single people.   Single people—working or in further education—should benefit from various measures proposed in the Green Paper for improving the supply of and access to housing. Subject to availability of resources, local authorities should ensure that adequate accommodation for single people is included in their general investment provision (12.48–12.49).

72.   Mobile workers.   Many of the policies which will help single people will also help mobile workers. Local authorities can also improve their arrangements for transfers and exchanges (12.50–12.54).

73.   Ethnic minorities.   The Government will ensure that special problems faced by ethnic minorities are taken fully into account in housing policies and programmes, in consultation with the new Commission for Racial Equality (12.59).

74.   Inner cities.   The need to make a greater impact on the problems of the inner city areas has shaped many of the proposals included in the national housing policy outlined in Chapter 6. In particular, the development of local housing strategies will enable inner city authorities to look at their housing needs as a whole—as part of a wider strategy for regeneration—and the arrangements for public sector housing investment and subsidy will ensure that high priority is given to inner city areas with severe housing problems (13.11–13.14).

14.04   Legislation would be required to implement certain proposals listed above and might be required for certain others: i.e. 9, 10, 11, 16, 20, 21, 22, 24, 25, 29, 30, 33, 35, 36, 37, 38, 41, 43, 44, 45, 46, 52, 57, 58, 59, 65, 66 and 69.

Scope of the Review, Advice and Evidence

Scope of the Review

1.   The terms of reference with which the Review started were:

To review the arrangements for finance for the provision of housing, and the assistance, direct and indirect, given from public funds; to consider what changes are desirable to facilitate adequate, timely and economical provision to meet differing needs with reasonable freedom of choice, and to secure a more equitable and balanced distribution of assistance; and to make recommendations.

The scope of the Review was subsequently widened to include fuller considera-tion of social aspects of housing policy.

2.   The supply of land for house-building and the location of new develop-ment, the organisation of the house-building industry, and technical questions of housing design and construction were not considered in detail in the Review. Work on these matters continues within the Department of the Environment and the Welsh Office.

Advice

3.   An Advisory Group of housing experts from outside Government was established early in 1975 to advise the Secretary of State for the Environment on the conduct of the Review and to discuss the major issues with Ministers and officials. The members of this Group, who served in a personal and not a repre-sentative capacity, are listed in Appendix 1.

4.   Studies of specific topics were undertaken by other groups with members drawn from outside Government:

—One group looked at possible ways of making mortgages available to people who cannot obtain them under present arrangements, even though their incomes over their lifetimes are likely to be sufficient to enable them to afford home ownership;

—Another group looked at the scope for encouraging new forms of tenure;

—Two members of the latter group also made a study of the scope for the leasing of privately owned property by local authorities and housing associations.

The membership of these groups is given in Appendix 2. Their work has been taken into account by the Government in framing the proposals put forward in the Green Paper.

5.   The Review has also taken into account the results so far available of the work of the Housing Services Advisory Group. This group, whose members include local authority members and officers, representatives of the voluntary

housing movement and others with special knowledge of housing, was set up in 1975 to consider the field which housing services in the public sector should embrace, and to examine and provide guidance on the handling of specific issues. Its work will continue after the completion of the Housing Policy Review.

Evidence

6. A great deal of evidence has been submitted to the Department of the Environment during the course of the Review by many non-Government bodies and individuals. A list of the main submissions received is given in Appendix 3. The various suggestions made in these submissions have all been considered, and have helped to ensure that the Review has examined a wide range of approaches to housing problems.

Housing Policy Review Advisory Group

1. The Group was chaired by the Secretary of State for the Environment and attended by the Minister for Housing and Construction, the Parliamentary Under Secretary of State for Wales, and officials of the Department of the Environment.

2. The non-Government members of the Group were:—

Mr John Coward, OBE—Director of the Notting Hill Housing Trust;

Professor Barry Cullingworth—Chairman of the Advisory Committee on Rent Rebates and Rent Allowances; Vice-Chairman of the Scottish Housing Advisory Committee;

Professor C D Foster—Professor of Economics at the London School of Economics; Director of the Centre for Environmental Studies; Special Economic Consultant to the Secretary of State for the Environment, 1974–76;

Mr Kevin Gould—formerly Leeds City Councillor and Chairman of the Housing Committee of the Association of Municipal Authorities;

Mr Michael Harloe—Centre for Environmental Studies;

Councillor Mrs Patricia Hollis—Chairman of the Housing Committee, Norwich City Council;

Sir Frank Layfield, QC—Chairman of the Committee of Inquiry into Local Government Finance, 1974–76;

Councillor John Mills—Deputy Leader of the Council, London Borough of Camden; Chairman of the Housing and Works Committee, London Boroughs Association; Vice-Chairman of the Housing Committee of the Association of Municipal Authorities;

Professor A A Nevitt—Professor of Social Administration at the London School of Economics;

Mr J R L Potter—Chairman of the Halifax Building Society; Chairman of the Council of the Building Societies Association, 1975–77;

Mr David Seligman—Chairman of the Planning and Development Committee, Cardiff City Council, 1974–76;

Mr H G Simpson, OBE—Controller of Housing for the Greater London Council;

Mr Peter Trench, CBE—Chairman of Y J Lovell (Holdings) Ltd; a Director of the Nationwide Building Society;

Mr R K Wilkinson—Reader in Economics, Sheffield University;

Mr J Wolkind—Chief Executive, London Borough of Tower Hamlets.

APPENDIX 2

Other Advisory Groups

Working Group on new forms of social ownership and tenure

1. The Group was chaired by Mr Harold Campbell, then General Manager of Newlon Housing Trust, and had the following members:—

Mr J W Baker—Deputy Chief Executive, the Housing Corporation;

Mrs Monica Ferman—Secretary of the Fairhazel Co-operative;

Mr Robert Gardner—Chief General Manager, Bradford and Bingley Building Society;

Mr Michael Harloe—Centre for Environmental Studies;

Councillor Mrs Patricia Hollis—Chairman of the Housing Committee, Norwich City Council;

Mr J W Hughes—Chairman, Bracknell New Town Development Corporation;

Sir Dennis Pilcher, CBE—Chairman, Commission for the New Towns;

Mr H G Simpson, OBE—Controller of Housing for the Greater London Council;

Councillor Clive Wilkinson—Leader, Birmingham City Council, 1974–76;

Councillor Derek Wood—barrister;

and officials of the Department of the Environment.

Working Group on house purchase finance

2. The Group was chaired by Mr K T Barnett, then the Under Secretary in charge of Housing Directorate A at the Department of the Environment, and had the following members:—

Mr J R Adamson—Managing Director, William Leech (Builders) Ltd;

Mr M R L Cowan—Chairman of the Finance Committee, Nottinghamshire County Council, 1973–77;

Mr Robert Gardner—Chief General Manager, Bradford and Bingley Building Society;

Mr N P Hepworth—Director of Finance, London Borough of Croydon;

Mr P J Nicholson—Secretary-General, Committee of London Clearing Bankers;

Professor J R S Revell—Professor of Economics, University College of North Wales;

Mr Basil Robarts—Director, Norwich Union Insurance Group;

Councillor Clive Wilkinson—Leader, Birmingham City Council, 1974–76;

and officials of the Bank of England, Registry of Friendly Societies, Treasury, Scottish Development Department, and Department of the Environment.

3. A special study of the scope for leasing of private housing by local authorities was undertaken by Sir Dennis Pilcher and Councillor Derek Wood.

Evidence

The main submissions of evidence to the Review were received from the following:—

Association of Charity Officers

Association of District Councils

Basildon Council

Bristol Visual and Environmental Group

British Property Federation

Building Societies Association

Central Council for the Disabled

Centre for Urban and Regional Studies, University of Birmingham

Chartered Institute of Public Finance and Accountancy

Community Development Project Information and Intelligence Unit

East Dorset Ratepayers' Federation

Fabian Society

Harlow District Council Community Services Committee

House Builders' Federation

Housing Centre Trust

Labour Party National Executive Housing Sub-Committee

London Boroughs Association

London Borough of Islington

Manchester City Council

National House-building Council

North Hyde Park Residents' Association and South Headingley Community Association, Leeds

Paddington Federation of Tenants' and Residents' Associations

Parliamentary Labour Party (Housing and Construction Group)

Royal Borough of Windsor and Maidenhead

Royal Institution of Chartered Surveyors

Shelter

South Cambridgeshire District Council

Wealden District Council

Whitstable Ratepayers' and Residents' Association.

Statistical Tables

1. The tables in this Annex amplify and supplement the main statistical references in Chapters 3 and 4. Most of the tables have been selected from fuller material in the Technical Volume.

2. *Price basis.* The majority of the expenditure figures, both in the main text and in this Annex, are revalued to 1976/77 prices by reference to the consumers' expenditure deflator (i.e. estimated consumers' expenditure at outturn prices divided by the corresponding estimate of consumers' expenditure valued at 1970 prices). When a different price base has to be used, this is specified.

3. *Geographical basis.* Wherever possible, England and Wales figures are used, but in some cases figures for England and Wales are not available. The geographical basis of each table is specified.

4. *Definitions.* The following definitions of 'household' and 'dwelling' are used in the relevant tables:

—*Household:* two or more persons living together with common housekeeping, or a person living alone who is responsible for providing his or her own meals.

—*Dwelling:* a building, or part of a building, which provides structurally separate living accommodation.

5. Where appropriate, references to the Green Paper text are noted on the relevant tables.

List of Tables

1. International housing comparisons:

    (*a*) housing conditions;

    (*b*) gross fixed investment in housing.

2. Age distribution of the housing stock in 1975; England and Wales.

3. National balance of dwellings and households at five-year intervals, 1951–76; England and Wales.

4. Households in physically unsatisfactory houses, crowded, or sharing, 1951–76; England and Wales.

5. Annual housing starts, completions, and improvements by sector, 1967–76; England and Wales.

6. Household type, 1961 and 1976; England and Wales.

7. Social composition of housing tenures:

    (*a*) tenure by socio-economic groups;

    (*b*) tenure by income of head of household and wife.

8. Housing investment and assistance, 1969/70–1975/76; United Kingdom.

9. First year outgoings compared with incomes in the owner-occupied and public sectors in selected years, 1914–76; United Kingdom.

10. Interest rates for housing 1967–77.

11. Indices of house prices, land prices, and tender costs, 1967–76:

    (*a*) outturn prices;

    (*b*) real terms relative to the Retail Price Index (RPI).

12. Increases in average mortgage outgoings compared with increases in prices and earnings, 1967–76; United Kingdom.

13. Indices of average annual costs and payments per owner-occupied dwelling, 1967–76; United Kingdom:

    (*a*) outturn prices;

    (*b*) real terms relative to the RPI.

14. Building societies' new loans and net receipts, and housing starts, 1961–76; United Kingdom.

15. Building societies' net receipts: short-term variations, 1970–73; United Kingdom.

16. Increases in HRA costs per dwelling, and un-rebated rents (England and Wales) compared with prices and earnings.

17. Indices of Housing Revenue Account costs and local authority rents, 1967/68–1975/76; England and Wales:

   (a) outturn prices;

   (b) real terms relative to the RPI.

18. Ratios of rent to HRA outgoings, 1928/29–1975/76; England and Wales.

19. Public sector investment and assistance, 1969/70–1975/76; England and Wales.

TABLE 1

INTERNATIONAL HOUSING COMPARISONS

(a) Housing Conditions

		Average Number of Persons per Room	Proportion of Dwellings with Bath or Shower (per cent)	Proportion of Dwellings with Flush Toilet (per cent)
Australia	(1971)	0·7	N.A.	89·5
Austria	(1970)	1·1	54·5(a)	N.A.
Canada	(1971)	0·6	89·8(b)	94·3
Denmark	(1970)	0·8	63·4(c)	96·2
France	(1968)	0·9	48·9	51·8
Germany (Federal Republic)	(1972)	0·7	82·4	94·2
Italy	(1971)	0·9	28·9(d)	79·1
Norway	(1970)	0·8	45·2(e)	71·8
New Zealand	(1971)	0·7	98·1(f)	97·1
United States	(1970)	0·6	95·0	96·0
Japan	(1970)	1·0	65·6(g)	N.A.
Great Britain	(1971)	0·6	90·9	98·9

Notes: (a) 1970; (b) 1967; (c) 1965; (d) 1961; (e) 1960; (f) 1966; (g) 1968.

[Chapter 3, paragraph 3.01]

(b) Gross Fixed Investment in Housing

	Gross Fixed Investment in Housing as per cent of GDP	Year to which Figures Relate
Australia	4·6	1974
Belgium	6·2	1975
Canada	4·9	1974
Denmark	5·5	1974
France	7·2	1975
Germany (Federal Republic)	5·3	1974
Italy	6·7	1975
Japan	8·4	1973
Netherlands	5·3	1975
Norway	3·6	1975
Sweden	4·2	1975
United States	2·7	1975
United Kingdom	4·4	1975

Note: Not all definitions used are exactly comparable.

TABLE 2
AGE DISTRIBUTION OF THE HOUSING STOCK IN 1975: ENGLAND AND WALES
(million dwellings)

	Owner-occupied	Local Authorities and New Towns	Private Landlords and Miscellaneous	Total
Pre-1914	3·4 (34%)	0·3 (6%)	2·2 (76%)	5·9 (33%)
1914–44	2·7 (28%)	1·2 (23%)	0·3 (10%)	4·2 (23%)
1945 and after	3·8 (38%)	3·7 (71%)	0·4 (14%)	7·9 (44%)
Total	9·9	5·2	2·9	18·0

[Chapter 3, paragraph 3.04]

TABLE 3
NATIONAL BALANCE OF DWELLINGS AND HOUSEHOLDS, AT FIVE–YEAR INTERVALS 1951–76; ENGLAND AND WALES

	1951	1956	1961	1966	1971	1976
Dwellings	12·5	13·7	14·6	15·8	17·0	18·1
Households ...	13·3	14·0	14·7	15·9	16·8	17·6
Balance	−0·8	−0·3	−0·1	−0·1	+0·2	+0·5

[Chapter 3, paragraph 3.05]

TABLE 4
HOUSEHOLDS IN PHYSICALLY UNSATISFACTORY HOUSES, CROWDED, OR SHARING, 1951–76; ENGLAND AND WALES
(thousands)

	1951	1961	1971	1976
Multi-person households sharing	1,442	582	380	275(a)
One-person households sharing ...	430	448	440	375(a)
Concealed households(b) ...	935	702	426	360(a)
Crowded households(c)	664	415	226	150(a)
Occupiers of dwellings that are unfit and/or lacking one or more basic amenities	7,500	4,700	2,850	1,650
Total (rounded)	11,000	6,800	4,300	2,800(a)
Total free of duplication(d) ...	9,700	6,400	4,100	2,700(a)
Unduplicated total as % of all households plus concealed households	69	42	24	15(a)

Notes:
(a) Estimate.
(b) Married couples or one parent families living as part of another household.
(c) At densities above 1½ persons per room.
(d) Duplication in sharing households who are crowded; and sharing households in unfit or substandard dwellings.

[Chapter 3, paragraph 3.07]

TABLE 5

ANNUAL HOUSING STARTS, COMPLETIONS AND IMPROVEMENTS BY SECTOR 1967-76 (ENGLAND AND WALES)

(percentages in brackets)

Housing Starts

	Private sector	LA including New Towns	Housing Associations and Government Departments	Total
1967	225,389 (56%)	167,208 (41%)	10,976 (3%)	403,573
1968	190,132 (54%)	148,549 (43%)	11,258 (3%)	349,939
1969	158,195 (52%)	134,074 (44%)	11,381 (4%)	303,650
1970	156,930 (56%)	114,778 (40%)	10,701 (4%)	282,409
1971	195,516 (63%)	101,600 (33%)	12,919 (4%)	310,035
1972	214,315 (67%)	90,855 (29%)	12,308 (4%)	317,478
1973	200,155 (68%)	83,871 (28%)	11,636 (4%)	295,662
1974	95,673 (43%)	111,397 (51%)	12,476 (6%)	219,546
1975	137,163 (47%)	134,302 (46%)	19,775 (7%)	291,240
1976	138,347 (47%)	126,509 (43%)	29,670 (10%)	294,526

Completions

	Private sector	LA including New Towns	Housing Associations and Government Departments	Total
1967	192,940 (33%)	159,347 (44%)	10,611 (3%)	362,898
1968	213,273 (57%)	148,049 (40%)	10,404 (3%)	371,726
1969	173,377 (54%)	139,850 (43%)	10,938 (3%)	324,165
1970	162,084 (53%)	134,874 (44%)	10,308 (3%)	307,266
1971	179,998 (58%)	117,215 (38%)	12,563 (4%)	309,776
1972	184,622 (64%)	93,635 (33%)	9,037 (3%)	287,294
1973	174,413 (66%)	79,289 (30%)	10,345 (4%)	264,047
1974	129,626 (54%)	99,423 (41%)	12,124 (5%)	241,173
1975	140,381 (50%)	122,857 (44%)	15,456 (6%)	278,694
1976	138,477 (50%)	124,152 (45%)	16,031 (5%)	278,660

Improvement Grants Approved

	Private sector	LA including New Towns	(housing associations)	Total
1967	82,622 (73%)	28,808 (25%)	1,712 (2%)	113,142
1968	81,126 (71%)	31,031 (27%)	2,059 (2%)	114,216
1969	76,384 (70%)	29,369 (27%)	3,185 (3%)	108,938
1970	110,533 (71%)	41,960 (27%)	4,064 (2%)	156,557
1971	136,175 (66%)	61,138 (31%)	6,168 (3%)	197,481
1972	208,415 (65%)	103,998 (33%)	6,756 (2%)	319,167
1973	237,976 (66%)	117,927 (33%)	5,051 (1%)	360,954
1974	149,290 (65%)	77,333 (33%)	5,295 (2%)	231,918
1975	84,504 (67%)	37,106 (29%)	5,278 (4%)	126,888
1976	72,762 (58%)	39,001 (31%)	13,868 (11%)	125,631

TABLE 6

HOUSEHOLD TYPE, 1961 AND 1976: ENGLAND AND WALES

(thousands)

	1961	1976 (est)	Change
Married couple households	10,489	11,554	+1,065
One parent households(a)	1,012	1,208	+ 196
One person households:			
Under 30	70	274	+ 204
30–59/64(b)	705	1,077	+ 372
60/65 or over	1,334	2,581	+1,247
Total	2,109	3,932	+1,823
Other households(c) ...			
Head under age 30	48	163	+ 115
Others	1,066	718	− 348
All households	14,724	17,574	+2,850

Note:

(a) Not all of these households include dependent children.

(b) 30–59 for women, 30–64 for men.

(c) Households comprising two or more people, none of whom is related as husband and wife or parent and child.

[Chapter 3, paragraph 3.20]

TABLE 7

SOCIAL COMPOSITION OF HOUSING TENURES IN 1971; ENGLAND AND WALES

(a) Tenure by Socio-Economic Group

(percentages)

	Home Owner	Rented from Local Authority, NT	Rented Unfurnished from Private Landlord	Rented Furnished from Private Landlord	Rented With Job/ Business	All Tenures
Professional occupations, employers, managers ...	26·9	4·7	9·6	13	25	18·0
Intermediate and junior non-manual ...	22·9	12·3	19·0	34	20	19·6
Skilled manual(*) and own account non-professional	30·7	40·1	32·3	20	25	33·0
Semi-skilled manual and personal service	12·2	28·3	25·1	14	22	18·9
Unskilled manual ...	2·9	12·1	10·4	7	1	6·5
Others(†)	4·4	2·6	3·5	12	6	4·1
Total	100·0	100·0	100·0	100	100	100·0
Total ('000) ...	8,228	4,628	2,246	550	750	16,434

Notes: (*) Includes foremen and supervisors.

(†) Includes servicemen, students, householders with no past or previous occupation or with undefined occupation.

(b) Tenure by Income of Head of Household and Wife

(percentages)

	Home Owners		Local Authority and New Town Tenants		Renting Unfurnished from Private Landlord	
	Economically active head	Economically inactive head	Economically active head	Economically inactive head	Economically active head	Economically inactive head
INCOME:						
Under £1,000 ...	1·5	34·5	1·8	48·9	4·2	56·8
£1,000– ...	2·5	27·6	5·4	38·4	10·2	25·6
£1,500– ...	3·7	17·1	8·9	9·0	10·0	11·6
£2,000– ...	7·0	4·2	12·5	1·6	11·5	2·5
£2,500– ...	9·5	5·8	14·1	1·6	14·2	2·1
£3,000– ...	25·7	4·9	28·6	0·5	23·4	1·3
£4,000– ...	21·2	2·5	19·2	—	16·5	—
£5,000– ...	12·6	1·2	6·8	—	6·6	—
£6,000– ...	16·3	2·1	2·6	—	3·4	—
Total	100·0	100·0	100·0	100·0	100·0	100·0
Sample Number ...	2,608	754	1,175	622	381	285

TABLE 8

HOUSING INVESTMENT AND ASSISTANCE(a), 1969-76; UNITED KINGDOM
£M 1976/77 Prices

	Home Ownership		Public Sector				Total	
	1. Invest- ment	2. Mort- gage Tax Relief (b)	3. Invest- ment	4. Subsidy exclud- ing RFC and Rent Rebate	5. Rate Fund Contri- bution	6. Rent Rebates	7. General Assis- tance (c)	8. Invest- ment
1969/70 ...	2,003	547	1,951	399	228	—	1,174	3,954
1970/71 ...	2,021	627	1,836	450	204	—	1,281	3,857
1971/72 ...	2,313	638	1,702	486	152	—	1,276	4,015
1972/73 ...	2,797	716	1,974	493	97	140	1,306	4,771
1973/74 ...	3,041	930	2,535	571	146	292	1,647	5,576
1974/75 ...	2,623	1,084	3,195	922	242	310	2,248	5,818
1975/76 ...	2,524	1,100	2,798	966	244	292	2,310	5,322

(a) Investment includes, in the public sector, capital expenditure on new building (including land), acquisition, and improvement of houses in Revenue Accounts; and, in the private sector, expenditure by home owners on the purchase of new homes, and grant aided improvements. Rent allowances are excluded.

(b) Includes Option Mortgage subsidy.

(c) The sum of columns 2, 4 and 5.

(d) Rent Rebates for 1971/72 and earlier years are included with rate fund contributions and subsidy.

[Chapter 4, paragraph 4.01]

TABLE 9

FIRST YEAR OUTGOINGS COMPARED WITH INCOMES IN THE OWNER-OCCUPIED AND PUBLIC SECTORS IN SELECTED YEARS 1914–1976; UNITED KINGDOM

	Pre-1914	1947	1970	1975	1976
Capital cost	£200–250	£1,400	£4,490	£9,450	£10,600
(A) Rental Basis					
Loan charges (60-year life, at 5 per cent before 1914, 3 per cent in 1947, 6·8 per cent in 1970, 9·8 per cent in 1975, 10·5 per cent in 1976)	£11–13	£51	£311	£929	£1,116
Upkeep, management, etc (a) ...	£2·50	£10	£85	£124	£140
Total annual cost	£13–16	£61	£356	£1,053	£1,256
Weekly cost	5s–6s	23s 6d	136s 11d	£20·25	£24·15
Average weekly earnings(b) ...	27s–34s	134s 2d	578s 2d	£59·74	£67·83
Cost rent as per cent of average earnings	18	18	24	34	36
(B) Purchase with 100 per cent mortgage					
Gross outgoings (25-year term)	—	£90	£425	£1,122	£1,213(d)
Tax relief(c)	—	£22	£119	£364	£390
Net mortgage outgoings ...	—	£68	£306	£758	£823
Gross outgoings as per cent of average weekly earnings ...	—	26	28	36	34

Notes:
(a) Average for all local authority dwellings in 1970 and 1975.
(b) Adult men in manual work in manufacturing.
(c) At standard rate less earned income relief in 1947 and 1970, and basic rate in 1975 and 1976.
(d) At 10½ per cent mortgage rate.

[Chapter 4, paragraph 4.12]

TABLE 10

INTEREST RATES FOR HOUSING 1967–77

(per cent)

	Local Authorities' Pool Rate of Interest (England & Wales)	BSA Recommended* Mortgage Rate
1967/68	5·6	7⅛
1968/69	6·2	7⅛–7⅝
1969/70	6·7	8½
1970/71	6·8	8½
1971/72	6·6	8½–8
1972/73	6·7	8 –8½
1973/74	8·1	9½–11
1974/75	9·5	11
1975/76	9·8	11
1976/77	10·5 (est)	10½–12¼

Note: Where more than one rate was in effect during the year, the extremes of the range are shown.

[Chapter 4, paragraph 4.12]

TABLE 11

INDICES OF HOUSE PRICES, LAND PRICES AND TENDER COSTS

(1967=100)

(a) Outturn Prices

	Land(a)	House prices(b)	Tender costs(c)	RPI
1967	100	100	100	100
1968	113	108	106	104·7
1969	141	113	110	110·3
1970	155	120	119	117·4
1971	175	139	134	128·4
1972	287	186	162	137·6
1973	458	249	224	150·1
1974	449	262	258	174·2
1975	318	287	283	216·4
1976	315	311	301	252·2

(b) In real terms relative to the RPI

	Land(a)	House prices(b)	Tender costs(c)
1967	100	100	100
1968	108	103	101
1969	128	102	100
1970	132	102	101
1971	136	108	104
1972	209	135	118
1973	305	166	149
1974	258	150	148
1975	147	133	131
1976	125	123	119

Notes:

(a) The price per plot of building land for private owners, England and Wales.

(b) The price of second-hand houses purchased with Building Society loans, UK.

(c) The tender costs for local authorities' traditionally-built one- and two-storey houses, England and Wales excluding Greater London.

[Chapter 4, paragraph 4.12]

148

TABLE 12

INCREASES IN AVERAGE MORTGAGE OUTGOINGS (UNITED KINGDOM) COMPARED WITH INCREASES IN PRICES AND EARNINGS 1967–76

	(A) Average Gross Mortgage Out-goings(a) (£)	(B) Average Mortgage Out-goings(b) (£)	(C) Per cent Increase in (A)	(D) Per cent Increase in (B)	(E) Increase in General Price level(c)	(F) Increase in Earn-ings(d)
1967/68	198	155	—	—	—	—
1968/69	213	167	+ 8	+ 8	+ 6	+ 8
1969/70	230	177	+ 8	+ 6	+ 5	+ 8
1970/71	249	188	+ 8	+ 6	+ 7	+13
1971/72	272	208	+ 9	+11(e)	+ 9	+11
1972/73	314	239	+15	+15	+ 7	+13
1973/74	395	294	+26	+23	+10	+13
1974/75	474	338	+20	+15	+18	+23
1975/76	546	378	+15	+12	+25	+24
1967/68 to 1971/72	—	—	+37	+34	+30	+48
1971/72 to 1975/76	—	—	+101	+82	+75	+96
1967/68 to 1975/76	—	—	+176	+144	+127	+186

Notes:

(a) Interest plus regular repayments of principal (including life assurance premiums).

(b) Gross mortgage outgoings less tax relief (including life assurance relief) and option mortgage subsidy.

(c) Index of retail prices.

(d) Department of Employment monthly index of average earnings of all employees.

(e) Increase in net outgoings greater than in gross outgoings owing to reduction of standard rate of income tax.

[Chapter 4, paragraph 4.16]

149

TABLE 13

INDICES OF AVERAGE ANNUAL COSTS AND PAYMENTS PER OWNER-OCCUPIED DWELLING 1967–76; UNITED KINGDOM

(a) Outturn Prices

	Total per dwelling	Net of tax relief and subsidy	Average earnings	RPI
1967/68	100	100	100	100
1968/69	108	108	107·8	105·6
1969/70	117	116	117·0	111·0
1970/71	128	124	132·0	119·0
1971/72	147	145	145·9	130·0
1972/73	170	168	165·4	139·2
1973/74	207	199	186·9	153·7
1974/75	241	225	229·6	181·3
1975/76	286	259	284·1	226·0

(b) In real terms relative to the RPI

	Total per dwelling	Net of tax relief and subsidy	Average earnings
1967/68	100	100	100
1968/69	102	102	102
1969/70	106	105	106
1970/71	108	104	111
1971/72	113	112	112
1972/73	122	121	119
1973/74	135	129	122
1974/75	133	124	127
1975/76	127	115	126

[Chapter 4, paragraph 4.16]

TABLE 14

BUILDING SOCIETIES' NEW LOANS AND NET RECEIPTS, AND HOUSING STARTS 1961–76: UNITED KINGDOM

	Building Societies' net receipts (£m, 1976/77 prices)	Number of new loans ('000s) (1961–64 approximate only)	Housing starts ('000s)
1961...	469	(295)	193
1962...	919	(325)	189
1963...	1,251	(415)	203
1964...	1,229	(445)	251
1965...	1,474	382	214
1966...	1,565	461	197
1967...	2,425	504	238
1968...	1,424	498	205
1969...	1,529	460	171
1970...	2,597	540	169
1971...	3,364	653	212
1972...	3,339	681	233
1973...	2,586	545	221
1974...	1,713	433	110
1975...	3,800	651	154
1976...	2,529	715	158

[Chapter 4, paragraphs 4.20, 4.22]

TABLE 15

BUILDING SOCIETIES' NET RECEIPTS: SHORT TERM VARIATIONS, 1970–73 UNITED KINGDOM

(£ million a month)

Period	Amount	Indicator of Changes in Competitiveness	Period	Amount	Indicator of Changes in Competitiveness
1970 Q 1	76	− 0·51	1974 Q 1	− 7	− 4·96
2	90	− 0·22	2	86	− 2·18
3	113	+ 0·99	3	129	− 1·59
4	125	+ 1·26	4	180	− 1·19
1971 Q 1	110	+ 0·86	1975 Q 1	243	− 0·30
2	122	+ 1·58	2	304	+ 1·37
3	151	+ 2·31	3	261	+ 0·48
4	183	+ 3·31	4	255	− 0·62
1972 Q 1	168	+ 2·90	1976 Q 1	348	+ 1·33
2	158	+ 2·68	2	229	+ 0·03
3	120	+ 0·06	3	176	− 1·46
4	155	+ 0·58	4	64	− 3·40
1973 Q 1	109	− 1·18	1977 Q 1	164	− 0·13
2	202	+ 0·19	April–May	(493)	+ 3·15
3	109	− 2·13			
4	84	− 3·48			

Note:
'Indicator of changes in competitiveness' is the Building Societies Association's recommended share rate grossed up at the standard or basic rate of income tax, *minus* the local authority 3-month deposit rate.

[Chapter 4, paragraph 4.21]

TABLE 16

INCREASES IN HRA COSTS PER DWELLING, AND UN-REBATED RENTS (ENGLAND AND WALES) COMPARED WITH PRICES AND EARNINGS.

	(A) HRA costs per Dwelling (£)	(B) Unrebated Rents (£)	(C) Per cent Increase in (A)	(D) Per cent Increase in (B)	(E) Increase in General Price Level	(F) Increase in Average Earnings
1967/68	134	94	...	...	...	...
1968/69	145	101	+ 8	+ 7	+ 6	+ 8
1969/70	161	106	+11	+ 5	+ 5	+ 8
1970/71	176	118	+ 9	+11	+ 7	+13
1971/72	189	127	+ 7	+ 8	+ 9	+11
1972/73	213	153	+13	+20	+ 7	+13
1973/74	253	178	+19	+16	+10	+13
1974/75	344	195	+36	+10	+18	+23
1975/76	409	223	+19	+14	+25	+24
1967/68 to 1971/72	...	...	+41	+35	+30	+46
1971/72 to 1975/76	...	...	+116	+76	+75	+96
1967/68 to 1975/76	...	...	+205	+137	+127	+186

Note:

Rents are average rent income per dwelling, un-rebated from 1972/73 onwards.

[Chapter 4, paragraph 4.23]

TABLE 17

INDICES OF HOUSING REVENUE ACCOUNT COSTS AND LOCAL AUTHORITY RENTS, 1967/68–1975/76; ENGLAND AND WALES

(a) Outturn Prices

	Unrebated rents	Rebated rents	HRA costs per dwelling	Average earnings	RPI
1967/68	100	...	100	100	100
1968/69	107	...	108	107·8	105·6
1969/70	113	...	120	117·0	111·0
1970/71	126	...	131	132·0	119·0
1971/72	135	131	141	145·9	130·0
1972/73	163	147	159	165·4	139·2
1973/74	189	153	188	186·9	153·7
1974/75	207	164	257	229·6	181·3
1975/76	237	188	305	284·1	226·0

(b) In real terms relative to the RPI

	Unrebated rents	Rebated rents	HRA costs per dwelling	Average earnings
1967/68	100	...	100	100
1968/69	101	...	102	102
1969/70	102	...	108	106
1970/71	106	...	110	111
1971/72	104	101	108	112
1972/73	117	106	114	119
1973/74	123	99	122	122
1974/75	114	90	142	127
1975/76	105	83	135	126

Note:

The figures in the two rent columns refer to total rent income divided by the number of dwellings in the HRA at mid year.

[Chapter 4, paragraph 4.23]

TABLE 18

RATIOS OF RENT TO HRA OUTGOINGS 1928/29–1975/76; ENGLAND AND WALES
(per cent)

	Gross Rents	Rents net of all Rebates
1928/29		54·5
1938/39		56·2
1948/49		60·6
1954/55		63·5
1959/60		71·8
1964/65(a)		74·3
1964/65(b)		73·2
1969/70		70·4
1970/71		71·7
1971/72		71·9
1972/73	76·8	69·4
1973/74	73·0	59·3
1974/75	59·7	47·1
1975/76	57·2	45·4

Notes:

(a) Up to 1964/65, rents other than of dwellings and miscellaneous HRA income are included with rents; 'rents' thus defined were then expressed as a percentage of total HRA outgoings.
(b) From 1964/65 onwards, rents are of dwellings only (but including charges for 'amenities'); and 'other rents' and 'other income' netted off HRA outgoings to show the amount to be raised from rents of dwellings, Exchequer subsidy, or rate fund contribution.

[Chapter 4, paragraph 4.24]

TABLE 19

PUBLIC SECTOR INVESTMENT AND ASSISTANCE, 1969/70–1975/76 ENGLAND AND WALES
(£m 1976/77 prices)

	Investment(a)	Subsidy excluding RFC and Rent Rebate	Rate Fund Contribution	Rent Rebates(b)
1969/70	1,540	307	132	—
1970/71	1,469	350	118	—
1971/72	1,370	381	78	—
1972/73	1,672	363	47	128
1973/74	2,144	421	108	263
1974/75	2,727	727	191	277
1975/76	2,367	776	199	259

Notes:

(a) Excludes Housing Associations, non-HRA investment, and expenditure by Government Departments.
(b) Rent Rebates for 1971/72 and earlier years are included with rate fund contributions and subsidy.

[Chapter 4, paragraphs 4.27, 4.28]

Contents of Technical Volume

Produced in England for Her Majesty's Stationery Office by Oyez Press Ltd. and Harrison & Sons (London) Ltd.

Dd 290786   K128   6/77